# MICHAEL J. CROFT

# The Harm of Doing Good

*A Study of Us*

This book was professionally typeset on Reedsy.
Find out more at reedsy.com

# Contents

# Dedication (Part I)

They say you should never meet your heroes.

# Foreword

God doesn't create chaos: he inherits it, and so do we. The moment our squirmy, slimy little bodies are delivered from the womb, we are born into a world of it. And over the course of our days we strive for order, routine, schedule, familiarity, happiness and rest. We yearn for better relationships with each other and the world we inhabit, constantly seeking to establish clear direction in the midst of the madness.

Yet our history is not the fable of perfection gone wrong that requires us putting right. It is not a tale of an Eden to be reimagined by mortal minds. It is not a paradise waiting to be recreated, by our hands or otherwise. The apple has been eaten. The bell has sounded. The song has been sung. What happened cannot be untasted, unheard or unserenaded. We stand as if on the brink of a void, into which every hope, dream, plan and promise evaporates and endlessly swirls in the nebulous fogs of doubt and despair.

For Chaos is pre-existent: it was never not there. It is abundant darkness, unmeasured depths; formless, shapeless and without rule. It is what abides before, between and beside Order. All we can ever do is seek to be orderly, while all around us the world grows ever more chaotic. And in the ways in which we have sought to be orderly, we have created societies, systems and structures; philosophies, politics and personas; cultures, classes and characters; figures, figureheads and fixtures; religions, relics and revelations; myths, magic and marvel. But one thing we have never done, and can never do, is reacquire perfection on our own terms. We haven't made it to utopia yet.

But still we try. We have always tried. We tend to think this is *good.*

# Prologue

There is a fundamental difference between being good and doing good. Being good is a state of mind, body and spirit; doing good is an undertaking of the conscious self. To *be* good, you abstain and avoid. To *do* good, you apply yourself and act.

When we ask a child if they are being good, what we really want to know is if they are keeping out of trouble. A child reading a book quietly in their room is much better than a child getting up to mischief and crayoning all over the paintwork or setting fire to the neighbour's shed. We hope that a child behaves for the childminder – not in the sense that we trust they will do the dishes, vacuum the stairs, tidy their room or complete all their homework, but simply that they will not be a pain in the backside. We'll take neutral over negative any day of the week. We don't usually ask if our children have done good; we ask if they've been good.

A successful day for an early years teacher is the children behaving themselves. The curriculum is irrelevant and the children don't care about it. Curriculum is invented by adults to do good for children, when all that truly matters is that the precious little souls survive each day by not maiming each other, and by developing into responsible, respectful, mindful teenagers and adults. If we think teaching young children is any more than this, or should be any more than this, we are wilfully blind. Or, we've forgotten what humanity is all about, and our place within it. For it takes a village to raise a child, but one bad child can raze an entire village.

Positive feedback for a child is that they didn't do anything naughty, not that they did anything particularly good. It's all about avoiding disaster, rather than setting out on a course to make a difference. If a child can deliberately not be bad; if they can consciously walk that indivisible line between order and chaos, then good will come of it. For choosing not to be bad is being good. This is the whole point. This is the crux of it all: both the fulcrum upon which everything is determined, and the vanishing point of all our endeavours. I could reliably end the book here, but then it wouldn't be much of a book.

Yet being good is not just for children only, but we only need to teach them to be good, by not being bad. This is the framework upon which all else in their life is built. From the earliest age possible they need to know what to avoid and what it feels like when they don't. And if they don't get to feel it, they won't know why to avoid it. For the risk is not the harm they may face and feel, but rather not facing it, or subsequently not feeling it. If a child has no remorse, the risk is exponential – for them, but mainly for everyone else. When they are not good, we shouldn't tell them *what* to do, but we must tell them that what they did was wrong, and hope that they choose not to do that thing again because it felt bad; or, at the very least, make a conscious effort to try and avoid it as much as possible. For chaos has to be courted in order for it to be thwarted. The rest they can figure out for themselves. We certainly don't need to teach them to do good – at least not in the way that we understand it, and especially not in the way we're doing it now, at such tender ages.

It is a dangerous thing to teach a child to do good when they don't know how to be good. If that framework of mindful abstention from being naughty is not constructed from the earliest stages of a child's development, there is no frame of reference for them when they are older. They will literally have to find their moral compass, but by this time it's largely too late. How can you look for something that should already be within you to help you find what you're looking for in the first place? Without a moral compass, you can't easily find a moral compass.

And at this point the good that they try and do will destroy everything. This is where we are right now. Society will go into a tailspin and everyone will be screaming – from every angle possible, at every opportunity, and from every platform that exists, real or imagined. In many respects, the sum total of our "good" is simply pointing out what we think is bad. We can point the finger and point the blame, while simultaneously missing the point completely. Our outrage will overtake our ability to work out why we're outraged in the first place, and if it really matters, because we have nothing solid to fall back on, and certainly no disciplined inner guide to provide direction, nuance, or reasoned debate. We will end up in a vicious cycle of believing we are doing good, but the manner in which we comport ourselves, and the stuff that we do, will not be unifying, orderly, collaborative, or mindful. In fact, it will be downright chaotic.

These concepts, and others, will be explored in the rest of the book, but to put it quite bluntly from the outset – our good is no good. It is harm. It is destruction. It is division, shame and loathing. It is populism, finger-pointing and outright nihilism. It is the end of us all, always has been, and always will be. How depressing.

And we are all part of this debacle. For these people are us. These people are you. It's our family, friends, leaders, followers. It's the whole kit and caboodle, as they say.

It's time to press Ctrl Alt Delete.

It's time to go back to school.

# Chapter 1: Green, Blue, Yellow, Red (Part I)

*May the table set before them become a snare; may it become a retribution and a trap.*

*Psalm 69:22*

In my days of primary school teaching there was a tendency to separate children into table groups denoted by colour. Not the colour of the children, I should hastily clarify. That would be educational apartheid. Who'd ever come up with such a horrifying plan.

At the bottom of the food chain would be the Green Group. Usually comprised of around 4 to 6 children, the Green Group would take the longest to finish, get the most distracted, produce the worst results. They were a raucous bunch. Likeable in many respects, but high maintenance and high impact. The children were a mixed bag of developmental, economic and social complications. A few of them would be utterly nasty. They'd have the most support in terms of learning assistants, but the least likelihood of academic ascendancy. There were always exceptions to rules of course, but the kids in the Green Group were, in a nutshell, predestined to struggle, and make everyone else join in. Expectations were low and small successes were celebrated with over-wrought joy.

The rest of the class knew the children in the Green Group – that is, they knew why they were there and that the Greens were difficult. It wasn't judgemental, it was the natural order, and they kept things transparent. If they had to describe them, they would use descriptors such as "naughty" or "always getting into trouble", or even, "not very nice". From an academic perspective, they'd be "bad at maths" or "not very good at reading". Simple yet effective generic terms used by children, but not by adults – at least not inside the staffroom, or in any official context.

It is somewhat ironic that one of our once safest places to express discontent, and offload the worst of our personal and professional frustrations without fear of castigation, are rooms now perforated by the subversion of self-righteousness and denunciation of perspective. If teachers were even allowed to describe their charges as naughty, it wasn't Government-authorised terminology, but it would be foolish to simply blame "Government" for such autocratic oversight. We abandoned the word naughty years ago – and many others like it – in favour of far more precious insignia. There was always a syndrome or a label that applied – an effort to mitigate responsibility for the negative behaviours and scholastic failings, and focus on the positives, whenever and wherever they could be coaxed out of the chaos. These children couldn't possibly be lazy, rude, obnoxious, naughty, cruel, thick or incompetent at basic tasks. They couldn't possibly be the product of a bad upbringing. And their parents couldn't possibly be the same. They were all victims of something and their behaviours were ours to manage, to placate, to tiptoe around; not necessarily – or even ever – to challenge. Instead of imposing order where it truly needed to be imposed, we became apologists for chaos and gave them a free rein. The Green Group might have only comprised no more than 20 per cent of my class, but they took up to 80 per cent of my time, effort, and emotional output. Maybe I was just a rubbish teacher. Maybe I didn't have enough help.

Meanwhile, in the Blue Group, things were a little less testy. Comprising a similar number of children than the Green Group, the Blues could be left on their own for the most part, but did need focusing and careful monitoring, lest they find themselves astray. A couple of Blues' members could be quite challenging, but did display flashes of conscience when confronted with a stern glance or a furrowed brow. Some of the Greens, however, took a teacher's bothered glare as an invitation to be even more of a gremlin. At least the Blues evidently weighed up their options, rather than opted immediately for carnage. Their wiring wasn't quite as faulty. Their neutrons followed some kind of coherent path. They were the ones who could go either way.

Next in line were the Yellow Group. 12 to 15 children of medium to high ability, and generally decent conduct. Even Yellows who were "bad at maths" – perhaps even bad enough to make them Blue – would not typically face such a downgrade because they were well-behaved. In their case, academic accomplishment would realise itself at some point, but their social skills, helpfulness, and cognizance of accountability, would ensure that they would always remain at least Yellow, in nearly all areas. We didn't have to worry about them. In fact, we pretty much let them get on with it. Thrust some worksheets in their direction and leave them alone for half an hour to settle disputes and manage the discord in the Green corner. After all, most of our time (and money) was spent over there. And it still is, in so many ways.

The Red Group – about 8 to 10 of them – built upon the successes of the Yellows, albeit more from an academic angle. Here were the high-flyers – the children upon whom the teacher could most rely to boost their statistics, at least ones that could be measured by Government. They excelled in most key areas – that is, to be quite frank, numeracy and literacy, as these were the key areas that needed the most attention, said Government, at some point. Yet with these two indubitably major tools, and a generally good dose of discipline, drive, and social dexterity, the Reds could pretty much tackle the rest of the curriculum with ease. History? No problem. Geography? Yes. Sciences? Of course. Art? Why not. The Reds could deal with it all, much like the Yellows, but their output improved the stats. Occasional Reds could be quite challenging in their own way, but that is always the nature of dealing with extremes.

The Reds and the Yellows, and most of the Blues (when they were focused), were the mainstream. Often certain behaviours and academic hiccups would place any of them at any point in time outside of the mainstream, but with minor corrections, effort and patience, they could all swim or float within it. Meanwhile, the Greens were largely outside of the mainstream – at worst getting themselves totally lost in winding tributaries; at best always tangled up in weeds at the riverbank. They couldn't grab a float and negotiate themselves down the river. Their independence was a liability. And while they were the minority in any class, the noise they made and the mess they caused soon drowned out the rest, to the point that they were the ones dictating the pace and the setting the precedents. Our lesson plans began to be built around them, and the rest had no choice but to accept it. And as this state of affairs cemented itself over time – let's say a quadruple of decades, give or take – it became the norm.

In a social context, as much as it happened in the classroom, the minority came to dictate the policies and procedures almost entirely by virtue of the attention that was afforded them. There is no other way of putting it. The squeaky wheel wasn't just getting the grease; it was getting its own, special garage. A safe place to be oiled.

If you've ever watched young children play ice hockey, they have a tendency to follow the puck, rather than the play. Following the play takes training, experience and, above all, patience. Patience with the game, patience with yourself. It is a natural learning experience and can only develop with time and age. Instrumental understanding gives way to experiential understanding, and that is one of the primal axioms of growing up. Despite the best of coaches, your Mini Mites will always be swarms of wobbly little skaters all chasing after the puck as their main focus, determined to get control of it and glide up the ice and score, where glory awaits. This is instrumental.

Yet from a teaching perspective, as much as a social one, we let the puck-chasers set the tone. We decided that a natural maturing process was no longer a thing. We figured that instrumental learning was bad, and opted to select the product ahead of the curve. But you can't make a fine whisky by faking it; you cannot rob the angel of its share and hope for a fine outcome. But we did. We chose not to believe in angels.

So we chose outcome over learning instead – as in, we removed the rote in favour of a tote – of solutions. Here you are. We've got this. Quick fixes for quick problems. We indulged our children in our own fallacies, and danced around their issues without ever really telling them they were lost in the fog. We encouraged them to chase the puck – anything to dissipate the tension, rather than explain it – and thereby abrogated (or rather abandoned) our responsibilities to their natural maturation. We cut short their course because we couldn't guarantee the end of it, and eliminated their obstacles to make ourselves feel better in the process. Their outcomes became theirs to choose at will, not accomplish through hard work and mental fortitude. We phased out uncertainty and phased in uniformity; the greater opportunity to thrive in a world of burgeoning convenient shortcuts. In the end, they didn't even need to think. We were doing it for them, even though it all amounted to thoughtlessness anyway.

Of course, the table colours I refer to in this chapter are as much metaphor as they were (and probably still are) actuality, and the children sitting at those tables are all of us, at any time. But it is evident in our society that regardless of our table colour, we often lack the tools to deal with even the most basic of problems. Our widely used, and electronically amplified resolution, is typically to cry foul. Even if it's just a pathetic and transitory meme, it's regularly the only mechanism we know. We didn't necessarily teach our children to be weak and have the attention span of a gnat; we didn't exactly provide them with reliable social or emotional engines to navigate the dangerous terrains inherent in simply being alive. We taught them to be unhappy with being unhappy, with no suggestion that their unhappiness was something created by their own choices in the first place. Our guilt became their fuel.

So when not happy with outcomes – when confronted with anything resembling peril – they demanded to dictate the laws and the litigation as well. Risk was evil, and exposure to it was unpardonable. If I am in danger, the reason I am in danger is because of you. And because of you, and the risk I perceive in you, the law must protect me from you. And if not the law, then any opinion I can solicit to back me up. With sufficient outcry, who even needs the law.

And so the law – slammed by an exclamation of objections, each distilled into pockets of mostly virtual and frankly surreal assumption – took a frightened and fleeting glance at the lessons of yesteryear and bowed almost unanimously in deference to their overtures. Ancient tenets were hastily swapped for more advantageous practices – ones that mollified the growing angst and swelling, all-pervasive rage. If we didn't like it, we changed it, regardless of the consequences. And if we couldn't change it, we interpreted it in our own image, and shoehorned it into our everyday realities anyway.

It may seem like it happened at once; it didn't. It took time, no doubt about it. All of this took many years. We didn't suddenly wake up to it, but a waking up process is always helpful. The hangover, however, is excruciating.

As laws changed, so did policies, and procedures, and ultimately sanctions. The far side of the spectrum was gaining traction because we were too busy throwing grit on their surface to notice that our own was lacking tread. It's not like we handed everything all at once to them, but we might as well have done. We even gave them relief from any contemplations we may have had to the contrary. To boil it down to thickest of syrups, we gave our gold to the revolutionaries, and they used it to purchase our petrified, concussed silence. We dared not tell them what we really thought. And we still don't – we bankrupted ourselves for this very outcome.

And thus, safely shielded from the calamity of opinions that frightened or frustrated them, clustered in little sanctuaries of intellectual bohemianism and self-saturation, the cacophony of their conjecture swelled without restraint, untempered by the acumen of antiquity, nor moderated by the reason and rationale of those few who stood opposed to the obliquity of their impromptu manifestos: declarations made without calibration or context, reinforced by little more than broadcasting noise. They didn't debate with their opponents – they yelled until their veins popped, and found themselves victims once again.

With crimes of perception and victimhood by-proxy now enshrined in law, airdropped on public services, educational establishments and all manner of other institutions, there was no escaping the entangling tentacles of this new, all-pervasive righteousness. Proof by assertion was typically the only proof they needed, and when any kind of proof was hard to come by, they simply made it up. They could, because, of course, they were right. And because they were right, they were good. Their defence, to them, is inarguable.

Yet as their own commotion multiplied, they had no choice but to shriek louder, as this was all they'd ever known. Crowds of them congregating around any emergent issue, jabbing at the air, swiping at each other; desperate to find tangibility and credibility in the midst of the chaos we had provided them. And when they found it – the puck of their chasing – they only had one goal, and it wasn't to pass. They had a goal, and they'd go for it irrespective of everything, even though they could very well be skating in the wrong direction. We let them free in the classroom and told them to take their pick. We gave them a choice of colourless tables and tried our best to guarantee end results, niftily avoiding anything that resembled the humbling rumble of culpability. This is society.

And as years went by, and so used to picking their choice of table, they decided the whole system was wrong, and always had been.  How could you even *think* about assigning me a table like you used to?  The fact this even used to happen is absolutely diabolical! That was racist! That's whatever word they want to use, regardless of the context and mindless of the circumstance – a pure premonition of the postmodern airbrushing of history now so apparent in their ballpark. If they scream loud enough and use sufficient percussive language, they will get the outcome, whatever that is supposed to be. Every day for them is Ground Zero and all that had come before was bad. Disagree with them, and you are wrong. There's no discussion, no debate.  You're just wrong.  And they can sit where they want, thank you very much. Petulance is but one by-product of extremism.

Slowly, yet inexorably, and with enough continued absorption and self-promotion, they would push the envelope even more to achieve their ultimate goal of choosing the proofs and the dishing out the punishments. Shame on all who disagreed with them.  Shame on those who decided their outcomes weren't valid or their suggestions incomplete.  They could only ever point blame, and only ever cry shame. It was more about what they didn't want or didn't like, rather than suggesting coherent or rational alternatives.  We hadn't provided them with the tools to do anything other than bleat.  And then we took the old sheepdog out to the barn and put him down, without any succession planning considered at all.

And this really wasn't the fault of the Greens.  After all, they weren't explicitly calling the shots. They didn't ask for all of our attention – we just thought they needed it.  At the very least, they needed something. But one way we let minority rule was because we were too scared and too preoccupied to realise that it was already beginning to happen, throughout the whole classroom. We spent so much time in the Green corner that we abandoned the rest. We set sail on a course that cannot easily be undone. We have exposed generations of children to the premise that the minority deserves all the attention, sets the tone, and the majority counts for nothing more than cursory acknowledgement. We have, in the process, enabled a society of screaming minorities and polarised, fractured group identities, and polluted the mainstream to the point where it is no longer considered the good place to be – in any context. If you want to be heard, you need to stand on the fringes and scream for attention, for that's what everyone else seems to be doing. When you let the minority set the tone, you abandon the framework that keeps everything together in the first place.

Our classrooms are a microcosm of our society at large. Each individual part of a group, part of a system. Each person with unique abilities – undeveloped, developing and developed – all at different stages, all at different times. In the classroom you didn't get to jump from the Blue Group to the Red Group overnight. It didn't work that way. While good behaviour wasn't always an indicator of academic achievement, at least being good kept you in the Yellows, well within the mainstream. If your numeracy skills took a downturn and the rest of your Yellow group surged ahead, you wouldn't be demoted – not as long as you kept your head down and your chin up, and showed that you were trying your hardest. This was all the achievement you needed at that stage. And unless you woke up one morning with Einstein-like intelligence, you weren't going to jump from Blue to Red in mathematics in a day. It took time, if at all. You worked to the best of your ability – that is, your ability to work. You might find yourself in Yellow for English and Red for maths, but never Green for one and Red for another.

Simply being good tempered drastic movement between groups and your overall achievement – educational and behavioural – was what determined your place at the table, and averaged you out among your peers. But when it came to eating lunch or play time, there were no table colours. You were all in this together. This is where the roughness of the Greens matched the frail sensibilities of the Reds, but the cerebral skills of the Reds (and the occasional budding A-type within the group) ultimately kept the Greens in their rightful place. This was where the Blues played like Yellows and the Yellows played like Blues (which was sometimes stressful for the teacher), yet all in all the academic, social and behavioural characteristics of any child would not dismantle or disorganise the group they were already in, and for good reason. It's why they were grouped that way in the first place. Even if little Ryan from the Green Group shared his toy nicely during play time, or sat quietly just like the rest during story time, it was reason to celebrate and congratulate, but he was still Green. And he would always be so. He didn't get to sit with the Reds because of this one, small accomplishment. Drastic movement between groups wasn't just unusual or unrealistic, it was dangerous. Nowadays, of course, we're disinclined to agree with such anti-liberal, non-inclusive racist statements. We can sit where we want, thank you very much.

A new child joining a class would be placed into a group. Reports on their educational and social background would follow them into the classroom, even as they made their first hesitant steps through the door. Their table colour was already waiting for them.

When a new child sat down at a table, in a group, it would shift the momentum. While the children in that group would be naturally welcoming, even in some ways oblivious, it would mean a change. A change to the seating structure at the very least. Sally might find herself with Tom still on her right and the new kid on her left. She was used to having Chloe on her left. This could be trouble, and this is where the teacher comes in. The teacher who gives the class a head's up and discusses with the relevant group, or groups, that change is coming. One child offers to befriend the newcomer and ensure that they learn the ropes and get a grasp of the local rules. Sally, who doesn't want to lose Chloe, but doesn't really care for Tom, offers to switch places. She now has Chloe on her right and Cameron on her left. A happy compromise. Tom doesn't care either way. A decision is made and it all works out fine. Fortunately – for everyone – the new child is Yellow. Even another Yellow, and perhaps a Red, could join the class at the same time and it would largely work out well. Discussions could take place and further compromises reached. The Yellows and Reds could work it all out. The Blues could be reasonably urged to agree.

Imagine now two new Greens starting in the same week, in the same class. The school had no choice but to accept them. The class is bulging at the seams and major disruption is afoot. One of the newbies is high impact. The other is almost beyond help. It's not just because they are unsettled, the poor little mites – but because they are also unsettling to everyone else. If you swing to the Left, you'll focus more on the "unsettled". If you swing to the Right, your concern shifts towards the "unsettling". Either way, it is now the role and responsibility of the teacher to spend even more time in the Green corner and request additional supports to moderate the risk.

Truth be told, we didn't support the Greens because we thought they would do well and thrive. We still don't, and we never will.  Not even the most self-deluding of liberal fools could truly support that argument on any kind of basis, not that they wouldn't crucify you on social media in an attempt to justify their purity of conviction. In fact, we did it to stop the Greens from getting worse, and prevent them – by any means possible – from disrupting the rest of the class who, sadly, by this time were mainly teaching themselves anyway, and slowly developing and consolidating their own minority behaviours. It was damage limitation, not damage eradication. And when the impecunious behaviour of the Greens couldn't actually be changed, it was frozen. We slowed down the decay with all of our effort, until such a time as we let them thaw slightly and move on to the next stage of their schooling. Or straight into jail, whichever institution was closest. By now, they were someone else's problem, and we had a whole new intake of Greens to mollycoddle. Rinse and repeat.

Unfortunately for us all, by the time we left school and threw our fragile selves into the arena of adult life – particularly nowadays – any such table-coloured restrictions or prohibitive monitoring was no longer acceptable. We are who we want to be, and we want to be what we want, where we want. We can move between groups at will, because there are no groups – or, rather, there *are* groups, but we choose to believe they are pariah. The end result is the same.

Many of us will be aware of that colleague who has been promoted ahead of their time – made a manager or a director when they lack the experience, skills and personality essentials of the role they find themselves in. Or, the employee handed a job solely because they hail from a specific background, or tick a particular diversity box. These situations, abundant in our modern workplaces, have no cogent societal foundation whatsoever. Societies have not been successful because the leaders (or, rather, the real decision-makers) were put there by some spurious make-believe policies. Not only do we focus on the wrong so-called positives, but we elevate such positives to heights they cannot sustain. For Ryan simply can't do the work in the Red Group. He's just not cut out for it. But by now, he thinks he deserves to sit there, and he's demanding concessions be made – just for him – and while the rest of the Reds disagree, a misguided Yellow stands in his corner, even if the rest of the Yellows disagree as well. (There are minority opinions within every group – i.e. whole point of this chapter.) The teacher doesn't have any say in the matter at all – politics is politics. Either way, Ryan is there, and he's backed by nothing more than a minority, and it's a gong show for everyone. And no one can demote him back to the Green table because no such policy exists. We never considered that part. We wouldn't dare try anyway, even if we could hear ourselves think above the clamour of innumerable opinions; or try and recuse ourselves from that kaleidoscopic monocle of disintegrated perspectives. We released the Kraken without a plan to rein it back in, while simultaneously convincing ourselves not to believe in monsters any more.

No policy, no matter how precious it looks on paper, can deny basic educational and social norms and structures. As such, these policies are the result of uneducated minds – the mindset of minority, anti-established rule. The minds of people who don't even seem to believe in educational or social norms and structures, and for whom such ideals are triggers. The same people, as mentioned earlier, who are also keen to screech out what they don't like and don't want, without ever coming up with a suitable, reasonable alternative. Welcome to the minds of people without an established framework, who don't just throw the baby out with the bathwater; they dismantle the whole bathroom and throw everything out wholesale, the culmination of which is more movements, more mobs and more madness – an absolute disregard and hatred for the past and the present, with no real program in mind for the future. Chaos has many bedfellows.

They think they are new under the sun, irrespective of all that has come before them. Yet the policies, behaviours, plans, tactics and mindset promoted and portrayed by these people are little more than the result of an attempt to do good – *our* attempt to do good – without actually *being* good.

That sentence is bigger than it looks.

# Chapter 2: Babble

*Now the whole world had one language and a common speech. As people moved eastward, they found a plain in Shinar and settled there.*

*They said to each other, "Come, let's make bricks and bake them thoroughly." They used brick instead of stone, and tar for mortar. Then they said, "Come, let us build ourselves a city, with a tower that reaches to the heavens, so that we may make a name for ourselves; otherwise we will be scattered over the face of the whole earth."*

*But the Lord came down to see the city and the tower the people were building. The Lord said, "If as one people speaking the same language they have begun to do this, then nothing they plan to do will be impossible for them. Come, let us go down and confuse their language so they will not understand each other."*

*So the Lord scattered them from there over all the earth, and they stopped building the city. That is why it was called Babel – because there the Lord confused the language of the whole world. From there the Lord scattered them over the face of the whole earth.*

This story from chapter 11, Book of Genesis, is known as The Tower of Babel.  It is not a tale unique to Judaism, or Christianity; variants of it can be found in offshoots such as Mormonism, in the writings of Islam, and in the Sumerian and Greek cultures.

In the Biblical version above, a central word in the whole text is "city", and it is easily overlooked. I would greatly prefer the story be known as The Tower of the City of Babel, rather than the commonly used truncated version. Either way, God frustrated the plan midway through construction, and so nations were founded via somewhat perturbed divine intervention. As an allegory, the story can be interpreted in multiple contexts, but one pertinent question to be examined is: *why would God do such a thing?* (With the question of his existence being utterly irrelevant to the existence of the question.)

Here we have humanity all working together, all speaking the same language, and getting along fine and dandy. They have an intention to create a monumental dwelling place for themselves; and within their dwelling place, an edifice to reach the heavens. Failure to accomplish this feat would result in remaining stateless, nationless; and being dispersed without boundaries across the face of the earth.

We haven't changed much. We also haven't given God much credit for his actions either. There is no indication in the story that God thought the plan was a terrible idea. Just maybe a bad idea at the time. He also gave us lowly mortals credit where credit appeared to be due, by implying that the venture would be possible under the circumstances, and may indeed have resulted in greater possibilities for humanity. After all, he surely wouldn't have intervened if he thought we couldn't have done it. Or would he? It all rather depends on what it was he was truly worried about, and whether or not we should all be worried about the same thing. Clearly we weren't worried enough at the time, when we started baking those bricks and mixing up that tar. And, perhaps most crucially of all, God's fear is most evident when he expresses that because we had *begun* our building project, then nothing we planned to do afterwards would be impossible.

He didn't step in as we were drawing up the blueprints. He stepped in when the bricks were in our hands and the tar was in our buckets, concerned about what blueprints may follow in the wake of our glorious towered city. And the only thing he did to scupper the entire project was to "confuse their language". Maybe Babel still survives somewhere; half baked, half done. I don't see any reference to thunderbolts from the sky or convenient earthquakes destroying it. Perhaps we can have another crack at construction when we all learn to speak the same language again?

Or maybe it's not the language that's the problem. Perhaps it's because we still don't – or won't – understand each other. For that's why God confused the language and that's what we don't understand. The how, where and when seem inconsequential to this particular legend. As for the *who* – well, that's you and I. It seems that our plan fell off the map. And plans are quite important.

One of the most powerful and penetrating questions we can ask someone who is suicidal, or demented, or simply disorganised, is whether or not they have a plan. *Have you got a plan?* It's also a hugely relevant question to those of us of sound mind, particularly those of us who think we are of sound mind – which is most of us, most of the time. To ask that question of a community, society or civilisation, however, may lead to rather opaque, or decidedly scary, responses.

Humans have always had plans. Babel was just one of them. In some respects, it is one of the earliest known plans. It is also an example – perhaps *the* example – of the human race all working together towards the same goal. That is, we wanted to live together in relative consensus, and we wanted to succeed. As far as I'm concerned, this seems like a darn good plan, at least on the face of it. But it looks like we may have focused on the outcome rather than the experience. We wanted to succeed (i.e. get to heaven) without sacrifice, and we are perhaps exemplifying this every single day of our lives.

Life is tough. It always has been and it always will be. It is full of risk and risky business. Every decision we make is not only an echo of the past, but a premonition of coming events. Our certainties are harsh; our uncertainties at best provide some hope. We will all die (this is harsh) but we may end up living a good, long life (this is hope). And this is about all we can hope for, some might say. Yet our conduct hasn't changed, despite the all-embracing myth that we are better and bigger and more advanced than our forebears. After all, weren't they bigots, racists, whoremongers, warlords, perverts, cons, cads and crooks? And those were just the politicians.

Past behaviour predicts future behaviour, as the saying goes, and I would add that present behaviour is well and truly predictable. For somewhere along the way we gave up on applying ourselves to the journey and instead pined for the destination, as the journey wasn't to our liking. We would much rather arrive at the outcome without uncertainty – without having to navigate our way through that thick grey fog of ethical and moral dilemma, where our choices might be held up to the blazing light of scrutiny, and where exposure of any kind was simply not something we would endure. Not that we couldn't endure it, but that we *wouldn't*. This was our decision. We wanted the city, the tower and the exaltation, but none of the cost. We wanted it quickly, cheaply, conveniently and, above all, on our own terms. We were building with assembly-line bricks of our making and baking, not with ancient and abiding stone hewn from the belly of the earth. Stone that took aeons to form by forces we could not possibly comprehend.

We experienced a prolapse of purpose, a decay of destiny. And it all culminated in a babbling rabble, which is pretty much where the buck stopped and didn't budge thereafter.

Imagine the haste, the heat and the hubbub. Untold thousands of souls all toiling on the same project, with the same dream and the same goal. Almost like a hive mind, their unity of purpose is unmatched in history and nothing, it appears, would stand in their way. Brick upon brick, layer upon layer: their city is forming right before their eyes and beneath their dusty feet, rising majestically from the plains; a pinnacle of prescience and prominence in a land hitherto unmarked with human enterprise and endeavour.

Then, as sudden as a sandstorm, they haven't got a clue what each other is saying. Scribes holding parchments of plans, staring in disbelief at their own markings, now completely unable to decipher them. Labourers halfway up ladders calling for more bricks, or more tar, being stared at hesitantly by workers on the ground: *did I just hear that right?* Friends joking during a break in the shade of an awning, finding their punchlines met with nervous laughter, each asking the other if they are OK, only to find that their words are the problem, their tongues not working properly. They stand, searching desperately for answers in each other's eyes, backing slowly away; and then they turn, calling, shouting, as the commotion around them intensifies; they join the throng, dropping tools and buckets, pushing through crowds hoping to hear words that make sense, words they can at least recognise, as even familiar faces are now no more than strangers.

A man trips on a bucket, tar spills into the sand. He's searching for his young daughter, sees her in the distance, standing still, as crowds surge around her. She is knocked over, no one helps. The man runs, pushing and shoving his way through the throng, arms flailing, yelling. He reaches his daughter and gathers her to his chest, saying her name over and over, hugging her tightly. *Father* she says, in a tongue he has never heard. To her, it's just *Father.* He turns, confused, but still holding his daughter like a vice, looking for his teenage son, who was last working on the far side of the city. His wife, as far as he knows, was baking bread in their tent just five minutes ago.

In the market square, chaos is unfolding. Scales once balanced are tipping strangely to one side, as patrons argue, appalled, as their customary purchases are suddenly skewed in alternate favour, and the vendors hastily rearrange the weights to try and mitigate the swelling angst, as stall to stall the common dissent spreads. An Elder tips a crate over, stands aloft, appealing for calm, for sense, as voices multiply around him in animated rage. He sees a peer, and calls out in recognition, hand outstretched in a gesture of beckoning, even as words beyond his understanding fill his ears with discordant clamor. The peer approaches, as the Elder invites, but the gesture is insulting, offensive, and the peer holds back, uncertain of his part. The Elder calls his name, but the sound he emits is harsh, like a put-down, and the peer waves his hand in decline. *I don't understand you ... you've lost your mind.* The Elder steps down from his impromptu perch, as tables are upturned, awnings sag, and souls rush in all directions with agitated intent. The peer is absorbed by the crowd, even as the market falls.

The man arrives at his tent, breathless, ducking beneath the door shade. His wife is standing, shocked, holding hot bread, and starts to jabber. He reaches towards her, pulls her arm, urging. She takes her daughter, asking for their son. He understands her, but their daughter starts to cry, confused, pained, and pulls away. At the entrance to the tent a young man appears, blood pouring from his ear. Their son. His father steps towards him, calling his name. The son recoils, touching at his ear, holding out his hand with bloodstained fingers, explaining the cost of his journey home, and the hasty alliances he made to do so, and why they should all heed his words and leave now. No time to lose. His father shakes his head, pleading, not understanding, grabbing his son by the shoulder to bring him inside. *No, Father.*

The daughter escapes her mother's arms and runs to her brother, understanding every word he says in his panicked outbursts, as he starts to gesticulate wildly, pointing outside, his voice raised in unbridled horror. Her father grabs her mid-route, she objects, her brother reacts and tries to take her hand. Mother intervenes, and they tussle, each tugging at the other, shouting, crying, words and pain and terror spilling out with every nonsensical syllable. The son falls backwards, swiped by his father, his lip now bloodied. Unintentional, but consequence prevails, and the son rises to his feet with loathing in his eyes, as outside he can hear yells and shouts in words he recognises: rallying cries of his new friends, a new destiny. He runs to his corner, skinny arms hastily reaching for clothes, his treasures, all he calls his own. His father steps towards him, tears rolling down his face, calls his name again. *No, Father,* says the son, in a meaningless tongue. His father shakes his head, falling to his knees, imploring, desperate, hands cupped in front of him in anguished conciliation. His son has all his worldly possessions assembled, and stares briefly into paternal eyes he once adored. *You never understood me anyway.* And he runs from the tent, lost forever.

His mother screams, faints, and their daughter bolts as well, dragged back by her father from beyond the threshold of their home. She wriggles and squirms, kicking, biting, but she will be controlled, and her fate is now sealed. She is part of this family and she will remain so, beaten into it, cowed into submission. She will not escape like her wayward brother. She will marry and bear children, whatever the cost.

All across the city, violent scuffles are breaking out over resources. A man staggers backwards, clutching his chest, heaving breaths and choking, bubbles of red foam spitting from his mouth. He drops a bag, loaves of bread tumble out onto the dusty ground. People swarm, jostle, gouge and kick. That food once freely shared is now life and death, as groups and clusters slink away into the gathering dusk, clutching all they could salvage or steal, as bodies of family and friends lay strewn on the sands in the shadow of the half-built tower, their spilled blood the colour of tar.

# Chapter 3: Risk

*You prepare a table for me in the presence of my enemies.*

*Psalm 23:5*

I f you've ever popped outside in your socks, you have taken a calculated risk. You may not have weighed up the risk to any great extent, but you nevertheless took the plunge and did it anyway. I can see you out there, carrying a bag of garbage up the garden path to the wheelie bin, or calling in the dog from your patio, or stacking up some lawn chairs at the end of a summer's eve. You don't always need to safely cover your feet when you leave your home, and you know this instinctively. How far you go without footwear is not typically pondered, as it's unlikely you'll give it all a second thought once safely back inside. The interaction with sock and soil is merely transitory. For you only planned to be out there for a moment, which is largely why you made that decision the first place. To you, it may not even seem like risk was ever part of the process. But it is. It always is.

Every decision you make, have ever made, and will ever make, contains a risk assessment. And every action you do, have ever done, or will ever do, contains an element of risk. For risk is inherent in all of life's choices and activities, so that we can somehow mitigate it and arrive at the conclusion or the consequence as safely as possible. For the most part, like wearing socks in the garden, the risk is minimal and barely even perceived. At other times, like getting married, changing jobs, moving home, having a baby, the risk is very much at the forefront of our minds – even if we are more consumed by the emotions we feel: nerves, excitement, happiness, relief. Nevertheless, the ever-present risk assessment and risk management is there, and it is but one part of our emotion's fuel.

When it comes to mitigating risk, we're all for the most part very good at it. After all, our own bodies are working their hardest to keep us trucking along without catastrophe, second by second, hour by hour, day by day. Our conscious thought is usually no different. And within our daily lives, the vast majority of our decisions are taking place within a very short time frame. We may be wondering about a decision we have to make in the future, but even as we contemplate that, we've already made multiple other decisions just to think about that looming choice in the first place.

We are risky creatures, some more than others, and the amount of risk we expose ourselves to is subject to so many variables and imponderables, it would be impossible to fully quantify. One thing we have become very adept at, however, is pointing out risk in others, and their actions, in order to mollify the harm they may come to, and the harm others may come to as a result of their actions, as well as make ourselves feel better in the process. A common method of mitigating risk, and therefore harm for others (and others in their vicinity) is to eliminate their choices or options in the first place. If you can't do something in a certain place, at a certain time, you'll be safe.

And so will everyone else. Job done.

An obvious example of this is smoking. Without doubt, it is risky to smoke. It also poses risk of harm to others. Over the last several decades, with some countries, cities and municipalities more ahead of the game than others, we have clearly not eliminated smoking: you can still buy tobacco products and smoke them, as they remain legal. However, by removing choices and options for smoking in various places, we have created a safe smoke-free paradise in our workplaces, parks, gardens, golf courses, balconies, restaurant patios and streets. We've done a whole lot of good in this regard.

And then we tried to deal with things like bullying using the same methodology. Surely if we can remove choices and options for bullying, then we can have that same paradise in our workplaces, schools and institutions. But how do you eliminate these choices and options? Well, you don't necessarily deal with the bullies directly. That's too old school. We make smoothies in the early morning nowadays, not shoot pistols at each other. And you can't make bullies themselves illegal – that's hardly a democratic-sounding ideal. The process has to involve everyone (without singling anyone out), and ensure that we all know what bullying is, and that we mustn't ever do it, so that it is eradicated wholesale, not person by person. You can't snipe bullying – it's got to be a wider social project and incorporate a bit more collateral damage in each delivery.

Yet our collective approach to issues such as bullying was indicative of a deeper malaise that we had tried our hardest to eradicate, using increasingly deformative approaches. If you choose to research definitions of racism, you will undoubtedly find quite a number of them. This depends on which country you live in, and whether or not you are examining criminal statutes, workplace policies, school policies, institutional policies, or more general definitions liberally scattered like seeds upon our conscientiously fertile landscape. You may find that you lack the inclination or the energy to even go there, and one can hardly blame you for that.

For quite a number of years we have rallied against the noxious and nefarious poison of racism in our midst. The risk of a racist society is something we simply cannot accept. If you missed the memo, you probably missed the training. If you weren't even aware there was a war against racism being waged in almost every structure and upon every platform – real or imagined – in just about every context you could possibly define, you missed rather a lot. That is, you missed a heck of a lot of noise, and an elemental change in socio-legal behaviour. We needed adjustment at a tectonic level.

There was not a single, precipitous event that signalled the dawn of our new virtue; our cutting-edge ethicality. It wasn't like a secret virus created in a lab, only to be unleashed on an unsuspecting universe when the time was ripe. But it might as well have been. There were certainly significant developments along the way that helped fuel the fires of our new holiness, even though there was no Patient Zero we could ever dissect and find the source of what truly created such tangential developments.

At the time of writing this book, it has been a couple of decades since a potent, enhanced definition of a racist incident emerged in the UK – the product of an influential inquiry into police actions following the horrific and heinous murder of a black teenager. Should you choose to research using some key words, you will have no trouble locating said inquiry. How much research you do, or don't do, is irrelevant to the outcome of the inquiry itself, as one of the "findings" put forth in relation to how a racist incident should be defined has, in many ways, proved beyond definition. Brace yourself, or not.

This new definition of a racist incident deferred to the perception of the victim, as opposed to the intent of the perpetrator. In many everyday circles, the preceding sentence may sound utterly innocuous. What follows isn't. Under this avant-garde rationale, a racist incident could be *any* incident *perceived* to be racist by the victim or any other person. Yet as somewhat normal (perhaps even reasonable) as this approach may sound nowadays to some people – it isn't. And it most decidedly wasn't at the time. The implications of this finding alone were monumental, and it wasn't even the smoking gun. But, again, it might as well have been. At this point, we seem to be beyond all reasonable or rational definitions of our own faults and flaws, irrespective of who claims to bring us a new one, and what research or review they conduct to make such a bold new redefining claim in the first place. Who even needs research nowadays.

And as far as racism goes, you can now safely associate other nasty behaviours such as bullying, harassment and causing offence. We somehow needed to redefine and repurpose them all in such a way as to offload the focus from how on earth we were going to prove such things, to how on earth anyone could say that they didn't happen. As such, we had to circumvent a rather ancient precept.

Proving *intent* has for time immemorial been a somewhat tricky aspect of an adversarial legal system, but a fundamentally essential element of it. But if, in some cases and contexts, we displace the need to do so, and shift the focus elsewhere, we make it a lot easier for ourselves. And so we did. We did it in spades.

If a victim (and, in some cases, any other person as well) perceives an incident to be a "crime" it is now a crime. We can safely bypass the need to prove it, as the proof lies in how it is discerned – not how it was delivered. The offence becomes complete and ready for trial in a neat and tidy package, eliminating any option for anyone else to say that it wasn't a crime in the first place, particularly those attempting to investigate it, or write it off as the nonsense that it typically was to begin with. This, by virtue of its own self-defining nature, enabled the creation of victims where no such victimhood had hitherto existed. We were all now able to claim victim status even if we didn't feel like we were a victim in the first place. We just had to say the words and lay claim to our designated and unwarranted misfortune. And others could even do it on our behalf. Society absorbed this by the spongeful, and gradually, incrementally, yet somehow willingly, failed to shake off the excess.

It wasn't really a tidal wave that vanquished us – more like a series of small but potent smoke bombs that slowly and inexorably overcame our ability to breathe, over a prolonged period of time. This was particularly evident for the majority; that is, the mainstream. But at this stage their voices of concern were beginning to be drowned out, and, in the end, their voices were simply silenced. It's always difficult to talk when you are struggling to inhale.

For years we have dismantled, disavowed and disenchanted our "front line", our mainstream work and social forces, leaving behind a residue of resentment, resignation and rejection, with fewer and fewer souls willing or able to stand on the solid middle ground of reason, as the obfuscating fogs of alternate beatitudes are wafted incessantly into their everyday realities, providing little more than a choking sense of over-perfumed surrender. If you've ever been forced to attend diversity courses, or participated in other mandatory "training" that aimed to make you into a better, nicer, more understanding person, by expunging all prejudicial inclinations from within your frontal lobes and correcting your pronouns along the way, you'll know that feeling well. For the new priests are in charge now, and they know what is good for us, and how to keep us all safe. And *they*, sadly, are *we* too.

In all of this, and more, we conflated risk with harm in such a manner as to undermine in almost unimaginable ways some of the most fundamentally crucial elements of peaceable and productive human co-existence. The substructure of our civilisation was now under threat from a new morality; one which would spread and seep its way not just into our halls, homes, classrooms, workplaces and institutions, but invade our consciousness to the point where it became almost impossible to think around it, or without it.

Risk is not harm, but we try and fuse them furiously together, creating in the process a staggering amount of erroneous justification as to why we do it, and why it is such a good idea. And those justifications become the new rules and regulations guiding practically every aspect of our waking, working and wistful existence.

I am rather partial to a nice cigar every now and again. Coupled with some decent Scotch, it's an hour or so of bliss. But if you demanded that I voluntarily fling myself out of an aeroplane at fifteen thousand feet with a parachute strapped to my back, I would quite possibly faint with fear at the prospect. At the very least I would kick you in the shins and run for the hills. My risks are not necessarily yours.

Whatever risks you choose to take in your life, you can't avoid risk in the first place. But you can avoid harm. Yet with risk *being* harm, your choices become rather limited and your outcome has already presented itself. Smoking = death. Marriage = domestic murder on standby. And as we continue to dress risk and harm together in the same clothes and present them as the same thing, we come up with not only bizarre policies, procedures and laws (as in, never seen before in the history of the human race), but considerably suffocating and dangerous ones to boot. It's a lot easier to justify the means, if you've already decided what the end is. We went from: *here's the risk, weigh up your options, make your decision, deal with the consequences,* to: *we've made the decision for you. Now comply.*

Treating risk as harm is perhaps no more evident than it is with how we treat our children. In befuddling both together, the harm is guaranteed to happen before it has happened, so we can't let the risk happen in the first place as they are synonymous. We must then restrict those harmful choices and options for our children – no more walking to school alone, no playing on the streets on their bicycles, no rough and tumble in the playground. (This is by no means an exhaustive list.) Certainly no old-fashioned playground games or traditional fairy tales that reinforce negative stereotypes, as this has already created a society of bigots, bullies and racists. You will not behave (or think) in this manner, for this *is* harm. You have no choice in the matter. *Comply.*

Eliminating risk by proscribing harmful actions and be-haviours (those actions and behaviours deemed harmful in our new righteousness) undermines personal choice and decision-making in a manner that leans more towards autocracy than autonomy. We are all suddenly destined to arrive at the safe outcome without ever having the opportunity to explore the risks. Yet risk creates learning, much of it through painful (and oft repeated) experience, but that is the story of the human race. It is who we were designed to be. God placed a naked man and a naked woman in a lovely garden and told them not to eat the forbidden fruit. That's risky. And frisky. It was almost like saying: *you have no choice but to have choice.* And that choice was risk incarnate; to not be presented with such choice is ungodly, in its most agnostic, fabled sense. We didn't get to where we are now because safe and beneficial outcomes were presented to us on our behalf and without our input, and we certainly won't get much further if we carry on believing that this is a good thing. Any society that has ever tried this has failed, or at the very least created and perpetuated misery beyond compare.

In our world nowadays, we can all have the same, safe results. Belief in equality of outcomes is one of the most jagged-edged, anti-academic, anti-human concepts of our time, yet still a mere by-product of our greater underlying angst, and always presented as a means to avoid harm, in its multifarious forms. But there is nothing new under the sun. If you think that this kind of behaviour sounds a wee bit communist (or socialist, or Marxist – take your pick), you would be quite correct. There are only so many ideologies to go round, and they will continue to go round, with all the "new" ones inevitably being rehashed versions of the old. And while risk = harm is not necessarily communism 101, by this very conflation, for example, you eliminate competition, in its broadest and largely anthropological meaning. If you can't compete (i.e. take risks), you can't make enemies. And if you can't make enemies, your enemies could never become your friends or allies, but your friends will always be your enemies, because there are always enemies. That risk never goes away. In short, you have no choices whatsoever, and you can only live in constant fear, forever looking over your shoulder for risks you know should be there, with no clear idea whatsoever of who is really who. The singular option is to capitulate to the rule. Obedience is required, and disobedience = death. And death may mean death in its stark, raw, real form, or the death of your career, or your motivation. It could be the death experienced when you are crucified on social media. (For as far as it is possible to conclude, crucifixions probably had a 100 per cent death rate.) Most pertinently, it would be the death of reason.

So as our children aged and attended universities, one of our great fallacies of conflation came to a rip-roaring, self-prophetic fulfillment. How our students ended up in safe spaces – safe from ideas, concepts or opinions is now perhaps not too difficult to see, but excruciatingly hard to digest. Watching them "de-platform" any speaker deemed to be a menace to their fragile sensibilities is no different to observing any other kind of autocratic rule in practical application, but the excuse is always the reduction or elimination of harm. And who would dare disagree with such immaculate conceptions? If you've ever tried to have a reasoned debate with anyone who has immolated themselves on this pyre of self-righteousness, you'll feel some sense of helplessness and hopelessness, even if you can't hear yourself think above the cacophony of their frenzied shrieks: *Shame on you! Shame on you!* The protest itself has become their blameless foundation. It's a one-dimensional, blinkered morality that presumes to tower above all else. It has silenced us, cowed us, and controlled us. It has become *the* morality. In many respects, it has become its own religion.

And that was always the risk.

# Chapter 4: Order



*Put your outdoor work in order and get your fields ready; after that,
build your house.*

*Proverbs 24:27*

Do you find that you do things in a particular order every
day? Yes, you do.

You do them because they bring you calm, quiet and
purpose. They mollify your angst, pay testament to your past,
and lead towards a more certain future.

We typically do not leap out of bed each morning desperately
looking for chaos, unless chaos has already presented itself in
the form of pyjama-clad children barging exuberantly into our
bedrooms, or our pets giving us a friendly, but determined nip
on the nose. We'll try and resolve those issues quickly before we
settle down again with a hot drink, slice of toast, or, for those
more energetic than others, a blended concoction of foodstuffs
with a slightly off-putting colour. Whatever our routine, at
whatever part of the day, our stamina is usually sufficient to
handle short bursts of chaos, as long as we can always get back
to our secure and steady sense of order. At other times, we
will make a deliberate effort to be even more mindful of the

importance of our simple daily conventions, and try to imbue them with an enhanced level of appreciative attention.

For the past several months I have been folding freshly-washed pillowcases, towels and socks in a singular way, placing them with reverent care into our closet. Some of you may know where this essential skill emanated from, but it doesn't matter if you have no idea what I'm talking about. It's not that this the *right* way, and failure to do so would lead to worldwide protests at laundry abuse and wider soft furnishing injustices, nor would it make you a bad person if you chose not to do it, but I'm sure our linens appreciate the tender and careful attention. It does the job, and gives me a slight, but temporary, sense of reflective satisfaction. I also drool significantly in my sleep and go through a lot of pillowcases each week. They deserve their special little ritual.

For this is order with a little "o" – not some grandiose, philosophical definition of the word, which any one of us could find such interpretations of in a click or two. The order that matters most in our daily lives is this little "o" – the order in which things happen, should happen, have happened, could happen, and happen whether we like it or not, no matter how much we feel like beating our tiny fists against a greater, immutable chest. Being orderly encompasses all of these things, and recognises its presence in every single thing that we do, every day of our lives. If we don't, can't or won't, we are in chaos.

Order is inherent in everything: the cutlery on your table, the calendar on your desk, the curl of a tail, the cry of a newborn, the clock on your wall, the catch of a ball, a clap of thunder. It is also present where we do not want it: the cracks in our concrete, the cataracts in our eyes, the cancer in our cells. Everything has an order, in order for everything else. All of our rituals (whether religious or not, because we do lots of things religiously) are simply doing certain things in a particular order, usually at specific times, for reasons we cannot always explain. This is a rough template, but can be transposed onto other contexts. There is little difference, at a primitive level, to preparing plates of food for the gods, or arranging the cushions on your sofa in a way that brings you contentment. We do these things in an orderly way, often for purposes we are at a loss to fully elucidate. We do them "because", and that because is our innate passion for order. We don't come up with schedules, rotas, itineraries, diaries, calendars and agendas for the fun of it. We do these things to keep chaos at bay. The same is true for our rituals, rites and religious rules, irrespective of our upbringing, or personal choices with respect to the divine or the arcane. We love a nice bit of order; we are hardwired this way.

For some people, when things happen unexpectedly outside of a familiar schedule, it throws them into a tailspin. In reality, that is most of us, much of the time. When I was substitute teaching in a new class, one of the first questions I asked my young, unfamiliar charges, was how their day was typically organised. It would then often take at least twenty minutes for the children to describe how things should be done, inevitably at the most intricate and bewildering level of detail: which child is responsible for delivering the class register on a Tuesday, but only if various other criteria are met, and whether or not it's projected to be indoor play due to rain during First Break, and then it's the responsibility of someone else. On Wednesdays the register is collected by a child from another class, but only if another child from a different class is present to accompany them, and only if they are not having an asthma attack. And so on.

Safe routines and schedules are essential for children. In fact, they crave them, as much as they crave rules and boundaries. They are also very keen at ensuring rules are enforced and things happen at exactly the time, and in the manner, that they should. That is, the order in which they are supposed to happen. As much as children are miniature bundles of energetic chaos, they know that this is not sustainable, and they compartmentalise those times when they are "allowed" to be chaotic, which is not always, and most definitely the exception to the rule. That rule is always the rule of order, in whatever ways those rules have been established in their little worlds. School is the prime example of such order, and where most of those rules abound. And it's the little things that are of utmost importance to little minds. Most of us can probably remember the disgust and dismay we felt when our break time was interrupted or delayed at school, for no other reason than the bad timekeeping of the teacher, or the naughtiness of a peer. Children can't enforce their own curriculum, but they will enforce the breaks so desperately needed from it. They, like we, need that order – always have, always will.

Doing things in order is not always relevant or realistic, however. We know this instinctively, but find it hard to let go of our familiar routines. There is always that sense of palpable relief when normality returns to an otherwise disrupted set of circumstances, no matter how old we are, or how adaptable and flexible we consider ourselves to be. For any kind of chaos, at even the most seemingly mundane level, does not give us cheer, confidence or continuity. We crave what our children crave, but it is most certainly not a childlike thing to do. In the same way that our children emerge from their play time to the classroom:

breathless, wound up, red-cheeked and often crying foul at the behaviours of their peers, we are also the same when we come in from the outside, as metaphorical as that is meant to sound. We all need to sit down on the carpet, put a finger on our lips, and listen quietly to a greater voice.

Our ordered lives and the schedules we create for ourselves are not necessarily effective or practical. We think we're pretty good at self-governance, once we've escaped the bounds of the classroom. But, really, we're awful at it. Every order needs to be monitored and, upon occasion, adjusted to account for issues beyond our control. Some things just ultimately end up being pointless, even if we could never quite put our finger on the point in the first place. Doing things simply for the sake of it, in a particular manner, are what we are all very good at, but, if we weren't doing one thing in a particular way for the sake of it, we'd be doing another. We can't stop ourselves in this regard. We will never stop striving for order. Ending one routine is never the end of routine. Order is always replaced with order. We cannot recuse ourselves from our own nature.

But it is also within our nature to believe that we can.

History is littered with some extraordinarily bad ideas. They're not difficult to identify. *What on earth were they thinking?* This is a much easier question for folks like us to ask nowadays instead of, say: *what on earth am I thinking?* Let alone: *what on earth do I think I am doing?*

We find ourselves in a rather ponderous position here, in these times. At our fingertips (or by a simple "hey") we can summon extraordinary magnitudes of data, facts, commentary and opinions instantly, all assembled somehow, somewhere, "online". We are so used to this word, we've forgotten that it wasn't one, not so long ago. But herein lies another complication – we can all learn what a word means, or what it used to mean, or what it could mean, but we can never truly feel what it meant to exist without that word, and without what it means to us now. It's very difficult to think as if with someone else's mind, at another time. It is also rather challenging to try and think as we once thought, without judging ourselves as to why we thought that way in the first place. Our customary self-assessment is: *wow, that was dumb.* We give ourselves little credit for our own maturity and experience, even though our future self will likely apply the same criticisms to how we are thinking right now. We also tend to levy that same critique towards others, particularly those figures in our past whose words and actions were so apparently worthy of our present-day adjudication, denial, or wholesale banishment from the history books. As the saying goes, we are indeed our own worst enemy.

History has happened in order. That is, quite literally, a chronological one – as cravenly simplistic as this sounds. Yet by the time "we" got round to adopting our current calendar less than 500 years ago (and not every country was on the same page for quite a number of years, and not every country nowadays uses said calendar), quite a lot of history had already happened, in varying records of time. Whatever the case, we have some construct of the time that has passed, is passing, and has yet to pass. We know intrinsically that there is order to be observed, and our very calendars are the results of observing order: celestial, seasonal, religious.

If we cannot humbly place ourselves within the time in which we live, our frame of reference is a narrowed, shrunken shell. We are also far less likely to be orderly. Accordingly, if we cherry-pick those aspects of our past to inform our blinkered contexts, we only serve to reinforce those cramped beliefs and opinions. We're very good at that – our personal information base is information bias, and we cannot excuse ourselves from our own perceptions, preconceptions and prejudices. It is only when we recognise and grasp this, our ability to reason and therefore be reasonable, is more likely. It does not guarantee it, but it sure helps it along. Reason is not order, but they do like to hold hands.

On a grand scale, our place within this order of history is infinitesimal. Our days are like grass – we bloom like a flower of the field; when the wind passes over, it vanishes, and its place remembers it no more. (You can thank another Psalm for this deflating commentary on how special we all are.) But we still have to fold pillowcases.

It is only when we revert to what we know to be the simple things, the sensible things, the rudimentary benchmarks of our now cluttered, crowded and confused continuance, that we may find within ourselves, and inherent in the world around us, a sense of calm, quiet order that is indispensable to our health, mental health, and other forms of health that we so erroneously and egregiously deny even exist. We seek order as much as we yearn for peace, and almost as much as we confuse the two.

For we don't have to float around on clouds, clothed in pure white garments, thrumming on harps and singing sweet eternal melodies to a nebulous, unknowable deity to be orderly, or peaceful. We're not very agile when it comes to extrapolating one from the other. We can waft as many purifying scents in our direction as we want, but they'll either knock us out or agitate our allergies, with maybe some milder reactions between those extremes, but beyond rewiring our brains through the hardest and ugliest of substances, we're not able to separate body and soul quite so conveniently. We can't find order simply by trying to be virtuous or ascetic or peaceful, and we'll only find chaos if we cross the line without a plan to come back – physically, mentally or spiritually.

You may not think that once you've finished your morning coffee you are about to establish a new social order; one that will swell and grow, accumulating followers, fans and fanatics, ultimately resulting in a "peaceful" coup that finds you sitting aloft some kind of ornate throne in charge of a small country. You're probably only halfway to the kitchen with an empty mug at this point, and that may come as some small relief. But we are also, at all times, those followers, fans and fanatics. We willingly allow, encourage and participate in, orders at all levels of society, particularly if we deem them peaceful, and clearly if we will derive benefit from them. We can accept the flaws in our routines if the routine itself is not dismantled, and confirmation is received that we'll be safe even if it is. For order is ours to command. It always has been. We are stewards of it, and can be terrible and tyrannical with it.

Order – of any kind – isn't peace. We must not conflate these two things as well. Order can be enforced; peace cannot, for this is not ours to command. We have created orders that stretch definitions of evil to the edges of all comprehension, irrespective of how benign and harmonious they have appeared, or how many times they have emerged and re-emerged throughout the centuries, as if by chance. We have recognised such evils down the ages, although we continue to recreate the very same orders under different banners, adopting new mantras, and altogether more deceptive packaging. But ultimately we are only deceiving ourselves. Our nature does not give in, give up, or give way, but we can give ourselves a chance. We need to have a handle on what it is we are doing, and try to discern why the little "o" is far more precious than it appears, with possibly no high fantasy pun intended anywhere in the vicinity of this sentence.

If creating a new world order after breakfast is not something you feel inclined towards, and you have no designs on exalting yourself up to status of governor, guru or god because you think you have a brand new conception of mortality (or morality) that everyone must be a part of whether they like it or not, then you are certainly within the mainstream. Your role, like mine, is not to procure peace through order at a social level, or promote order as peace itself. Your position is far more lowly. Mine certainly is – I have laundry to do.

We don't live in order to meticulously fold linens in an orderly way, but we may find that the smallest, simplest, purest of routines, gives us a glimpse of that grandiose illumination of Order that no click, "hey" or substance could ever substantially provide. The big picture isn't even a picture. It's a plan, and it's happening in order. That pillowcase may very well represent the fabric of our entire existence.

# Chapter 5: Gate



*Nehemiah 12:25*

(Matt, Babs, Oliver, Michelle, Tarek and Akim are uniformed and lightly armed security guards working rotational shifts on an industrial estate, for just above minimum wage, employed to safeguard the interests and assets of various business premises.)

A Gatekeeper stands at an ancient gate.  He is not expensively dressed, but his cloth is thickly woven and fit for purpose. He has a small signet ring on a finger, a symbol of his position, granted to him by an even more ancient order, and his role is evident to all who pass. His hat is a dead giveaway.

People come and go; the gate is opened and closed.  Some show parchment to the Gatekeeper, some don't. Some nod in respect, some barely give him the time of day. Some are turned away.

One such individual is objecting – he is trying to enter the gate, but the Gatekeeper is blocking his way. The man is agitated, causing a minor disturbance. Most people continue on with their business, others stop and watch. Some know why the man is being barred entry, others don't. Still others don't even care.

Suddenly, the man stumbles backwards, grazing his head on the rough ground. Was he pushed? The Gatekeeper may have done this, and the man immediately cries foul, imploring those around him with wild eyes for support, touching his tender scalp and holding up bloodied fingertips. No one helps. They just watch, but form instant opinions as to what exactly has just happened, and why.

You can probably see where this is going. Call him Mattaniah, or just Matt, a video of this interchange has been uploaded to social media within a few minutes, and gone viral within hours. Gatekeeper Matt is suspended from his job due to the virtual outcry.

We are never too far away from Babel.

An abundance of gates is very much representative of a conservative mindset. A libertarian mind, on the other hand, is rather more open plan. Gates that protect the sacred, the sacrosanct and the solemn would be more apparent with conservatism, while various forms of liberalist thinking may not necessarily have to pass through those kinds of gates – certainly not as many of them. Whatever our political or moral persuasion we all have gates, have had gates, want gates and don't want gates. It's a daily struggle – with each other, as much as it is with ourselves.

As Left and Right argue and antagonise each other across the political spectrum, and up and down the moral one, we're all very much concerned with those gates, even if we don't think we are. We project our gates, or our free empty spaces where no gates exist, like holograms into the world before us. To one set of eyes that free space represents a degeneration of respect, regard and reverence, and a lack of rules, boundaries and law; while to another set of eyes those gates are control, containment and custody, and an over-abundance of rules, boundaries and law. As my wife likes to say: *how it occurs to you is how it will be for you.* And when we don't like what we see, we vocalise, and how extraordinarily vocal we can be.

It is perhaps possible to sum up such disagreement and discord with two questions: *How can you have a gate there? How can you not have a gate there?* We can scream these opposing queries at each other all day, trying our hardest to make the other understand our point (and I recommend you yelling each of these to yourself, emphasising different words for maximum effect and trying to find your perfect version), but if we're missing a gate, or we're stuck behind one and refusing to open it, we're not going to get on that fabled "same page" territory so deeply sought after. We're not even going to be in the same pulp mill.

If you have a conservative mindset, and likely possess more gates to navigate through and project into the world around you when it comes to decision-making or your overall approach to life, you may find that getting castigated in regards to those gates of yours is becoming more and more common. It's possibly a little easier, say, for someone on the extreme Left of political or moral persuasion to focus on an existing gate and point out how obvious (and therefore how obviously wrong) it is, than it is for someone on the farther Right to focus on a gate that no longer exists, or never existed in the world of the extreme Left, particularly when attrition has had its way, and the amorphous, indeterminate blob of hard Leftist sensibilities seems to contain no handle or angle whatsoever. That doesn't stop the extreme Right from being screaming mad, of course – they are still all screaming. As such, we go back to the same two questions as earlier, just shrieked louder and with more vehemence, sometimes employing violence to drive the point home – whatever that point is meant to be. Something gate-related, no doubt. As to who is "winning" this war of polarised howling is anyone's guess, but without question there is cause for concern as to who, if anyone, is left standing watch at our most fundamental, constitutive and revered entryways. Matt certainly isn't. And neither are the shriekers.

From a social perspective, we seem to have largely lost sight of why we have gates, and why they must be guarded. It's not necessarily a deliberate assault on conservatism, but it might as well be. The end results and by-products of aggressive progressiveness aren't all nice and fluffy, even if it's all marketed as a comfort blanket for the social soul. Not having specific gates is simply damaging beyond repair, as much as some extremes of political mentality might take umbrage to such a statement.

A current proclivity to flinging as many gates as wide open as we can in a vain attempt to include everyone, at all times, for reasons of spurious justification, is unhinging and deconstructing that framework that keeps everything together in the first place. There's a whole lot of fencing and untold miles of ancient walls attached to some gates, and exposing those structures to disuse or disrepair can be dangerous, let alone devastating. Gates exist for a reason, and they are discriminatory for reasons beyond our collective understanding. Yet pointing out discrimination simply because it appears that way is what we do very, very well nowadays. Ask Matt.

Almost a quarter of a century ago I went for a teaching degree interview at a university in the UK. The old lecturer who was interviewing me enunciated something I have evidently never forgotten. He said, without fuss or fanfare: *education is all about frustrating children's minds.*

But we don't like frustration, any more than we like discrimination.  These words are like blue touch-paper to our sensibilities, along with others like them, and we have firmly decided that they are almost exclusively negative in essence, application and appearance.  In other words, we can't utilise them for good, or for learning, as they are inherently bad.  If they happen, in any situation, they are automatically pariah. Frustration = wrong. Discrimination = wrong. Remind you of something?

That being said, we don't tend to wake up in the morning singing songs of how great it is to be frustrated, or discriminated against. The overwhelming negativity of these words – and the all too obvious nefarious implications and applications of them – ensures that we assign them to the wastebin of our distaste and displeasure without further ado.  So we don't talk about frustrating children's minds, as that sounds rather egregious. We can't encourage that kind of harm. And discrimination is just a harmful word, full stop.

While my brief analysis above is admittedly rather clunky, it's one of the many reasons why we can be seen waving placards – literally and metaphorically – that cry for an end to this and an end to that. *End injustice. End inequality. End racism. End discrimination.* These declarations sound so worthy, and in the broadest and most holistic sense they are, but they are also exceedingly short-sighted, as well as extremely short, and lack any kind of planning.  They also hijack incredibly powerful, complex and emotive words, and use them as proofs to hammer home very large, square pegs into very small, round holes. Creating policies and procedures (and enforcing direct action) around statements as oversimplified as these is a blank cheque to authoritarianism. Gates exist for a reason.

We know by now that we'd much rather focus on safe and positive outcomes, so: inclusion = right. This doesn't mean that it is wrong, but we leave ourselves little room for nuance here, and the word itself has become symbolic of our holy social quest to fling open those horrible restrictive gates; those checkpoints of automatic disfavour. Context tends to evaporate rather quickly when the fires of self-righteousness are roaring. We wave inclusivity around like a flag, demanding that everyone rally to our cause, saying the same mantras over and over and over in that nobly firm, but all too lifeless and mechanical way. *We will not tolerate discrimination in our workplace. We are an open, inclusive organisation. Matt has been placed on leave without pay while we investigate this most serious allegation of discrimination and excessive use of force. We will not tolerate this kind of behaviour within our organisation. We are an open, inclusive workplace.* And on it goes. Maybe we got so "open" because we left too many gates that way. Trying to close them again is against policy.

Unfortunately for Matt, and a whole host of other gatekeepers, a bit of convenient amalgamation of ideas is going on, in order to justify the protest. The gatekeeper is being confused with the gate – one has become synonymous with the other, and if the gate itself is discrimination, then the gatekeeper only serves to represent and reinforce that negative consequence. The gatekeeper becomes the symbol of oppression and social injustice, even if they are not standing anywhere near a gate. Their very role will suffice. This is all too painfully obvious nowadays. It leaves very little room for nuance, reason, or, quite simply, common sense. It also limits (and now practically guarantees) our collective response to any kind of allegation or appearance of discrimination because, as we examined earlier, perception is now the proof. And what better proof than hundreds of thousands of views online, with many thousands forming the same angry mob opinion? The gavel has already struck the sounding block. Basically, Matt is screwed.

Our gatekeepers have done some pretty awful things through-out the years. There are bad apples in every batch, but they have very much become the focus of our ire, particularly when they do something blatantly atrocious. Or not. We like to pick on them anyway, and if possible goad them into doing whatever it is we are screaming at them not to do in the first place. Anything to prove our point and hold out those bloodied fingertips of ours in outrage, pain and disgust. Bad tactics are employed by all sides. Even better if we can spice things up with some accusations of discrimination based on race or colour. Or based on whatever we want. We've spent years creating enough fake reasons to be discriminated against, that we can find it everywhere and anywhere we look, even if we're not looking for it. Others can do it on our behalf, don't forget. Filtering out the facts from the noise has become next to impossible.

Yet as we continue to try and convince ourselves that we all deserve to pass through or dismantle whichever gate we want, whenever we want, because discrimination is basically always bad, we put ourselves more at risk, ironically enough, of a greater need to be discriminating, as we've lost many key frames of reference. That empty, ambiguous, unstructured space can be a difficult one to quantify and it almost certainly lacks coherence. And when things become so diluted that we can hardly discern how they used to be, or even should be, we end up using a lot of effort and energy to reintroduce some flavour, which means discriminatory choice as to what flavour we bring back. Order begets order, even among the disordered. But when we are in full-blown self-righteous mode, we never see ourselves as the discriminators, or as replacing one set of awful circumstances with another. Waging war on discrimination is simply waging war on our own nature. And that war is only getting worse.

Our world is neither a better nor safer place with many gates now wide open. We laid off those gatekeepers, or gave them desk jobs away from the front line. A few gatekeepers we had to send to prison – their crimes flash-points of protest, unrest and riot. It's not as if the mob need to be given such a fertile cause because they'll just make one up, but when the evidence is hard to refute, difficult to stomach, or so appalling, it spawns whole movements (fuelled with the power of the online world, the fecklessness of the media and our almost wholesale fickleness), we're in dangerous territory. It's not so much the disorder of the protest that is most concerning, it's the demands that are made, and all too often met, and the gates that are smashed from their ancient hinges, never to be replaced. Extreme behaviour results in extremely bad outcomes for everyone – perpetrator, agitator and observer. We're all in this unholy sludge together.

But we need to extricate ourselves from confusing gates with gatekeepers. We are all gatekeepers of our own thoughts, opinions and actions. Blaming one authority just because it is authority gets us nowhere very fast or very far, and holding up one gatekeeper's bad actions as representative of all authority only serves to create even more division, and lead to increasing unrest. If we made some small attempt to check out the integrity of our own gates and work out where they are, how well kept they are, and how they make us think (and feel), we might lean towards more valuable and productive discourse, and in the process drag ourselves collectively back from those extremes, where we can at least find the middle ground. It's more about picking our own brains than it is about picking a side.

However, if you search your mind and find no gates whatsoever, you probably didn't make it as far as this chapter anyway, let alone the front cover.

# Chapter 6: Vitae



*Folly brings joy to one who has no sense, but whoever has
understanding keeps a straight course.*

*Proverbs 15:21*

I would imagine that your curriculum vitae (aka your resume) exists somewhere in an electronic format. Somewhat forsaken are those days of printing them on lovely, high quality parchment-style paper, perhaps even paper containing a watermark to really enhance the specialness that is you. This may still be a thing – I have no idea – but if you wanted to be buried with your vitae, you'd either have to print it out, or stick it on a flash drive, with the latter option being rather an ignominious choice. Either way, you may never have considered this at all, and if your preferred means of preparation for eternal rest is cremation, this may very well preclude the flash drive option during the hot part. Again, I have no idea.

Vitae comes from the Latin *life* – the course of one's life or career.  Promoting and presenting the course of our mortal existence to date on two or three pieces of paper is no mean feat. Constant agonising tweaks and touch-ups are required, and we may never really feel completely satisfied with the final product, before we send it on its way through the airwaves or via the mailbox to the individual lucky enough to receive it. And as we gain more experience, education, training and cynicism, the updating part becomes even more of a pain. It's certainly not an enjoyable experience compressing the material of ourselves, and extrapolating the material from ourselves, into a neat and tidy little package.

So there will undoubtedly come a satisfying time when we stop physically updating our vitae. Retirement would perhaps be the first major milestone, and death the comprehensive and final one, albeit as dissatisfying as that outcome undoubtedly is. At least by the time we retire, however, our working and volunteer career – as well as all else that is inscribed as if with calligraphic elegance on that virtual goatskin of our condensed self – is mostly complete, at least from an employment-seeking point of view. This probably begs the question why anyone would want to be laid to rest with their vitae, but you never know. The way we tend to promote ourselves within them suggests a preciousness above that of gold, or any other cherished relic that might adorn our tomb. For some of us, in a sweetly ironic manner, they are the very hills we choose to die on. For it is perhaps not so common that our vitae is laid gently on our pallid, ghostly shell, or forms part of our ashy residue, as we have often already gone down in a blaze of glory holding onto it for dear life anyway.

Yet the very essence that is you cannot be encapsulated within a document, or an email, or text message, blog, biography or biopic. Whatever your medium of portrayal, you are way more than your vitae. Isn't it nice to be reminded of just how awesome you are? It's also nice to imagine poking the kinds of people who say such things in the eye. You're not awesome – your vitae is.

*You* are a pain in the backside, just like me.

We are masters of conflation, if that is not already evident by now, and there's plenty more of where that came from. We are a bottomless well of all things erroneous, out of context, and excessively random. The frivolity of modernity is not too hard to miss, or even avoid, but our vitae tend to transcend all of this. While some of us may opt for coy, cheeky, circumspect or even captain courageous in our vitae, they are in many respects the greatest unifying documents in our societies. For they are based on a template, some may even say a gate, and it's not one we typically mess around with. After all, self-promotion is a serious business.  Even some of the shriekers could be reasonably urged to agree, if we could stop them adjusting said template too much, or if we could even convince them that such a template even exists. The shrieking to reasoning transition is a tough one for all concerned.

Are we all good team players? Yes, in writing. In reality, not so much. And how about that comprehensive list of education and training? For some of us we have to exclude a fair amount just to keep the word count down. Others really need to scrape the barrel and get creative in this section. Whatever the case, the trajectory of our vitae is mostly linear: we started here, we went there, we did this, we're here now.  And we want to move on.  Although each vitae is personal and unique – that uniqueness of you still represents a broader, shared experience. There wouldn't be any point describing yourself as "unique" if you were the only person in the universe, and extremely unique people tend to think that they are anyway. The middle ground is more or less not very unique at all.

And it is this lack of uniqueness in the middle that is, it seems, all too unappealing these days. We have arrived – somehow, some way – at a place in our social history where being at the outskirts is now the norm, and something we are inclined towards more often than not. We appear to occupy the frayed and frazzled edges of our everyday existence more regularly than the secure, boring, sensible centre. The drudgery of life can evidently be spiced up with some "way out there" stuff, and that includes our own opinions and behaviours, as much as wider political activity and global online shenanigans. We are all very much out there, in all manner of contexts.

Yet our vitae don't reflect this. Yes, you can use a funky font, print it on unicorn-embossed paper and deliver it to a prospective employer by carrier pigeon, but you wouldn't be anywhere near even the outermost fringes of the mainstream if you did something like this. Your vitae is more closely guarded and sacrosanct than you may care to admit. And it almost certainly doesn't paint you as a placard-bearing agitator, masked thug, or generally lazy lout – even if you are all, or some, of those things sometimes. Our vitae is the best of us; the rest of us is typically the worst.

In an earlier chapter I made reference to my penchant for smoking cigars, as opposed to that utterly terrifying and un-necessary proclivity for leaping out of planes for fun. It's unlikely if I were presently updating my vitae that *admittedly excessive cigar smoking and hearty whisky consumption* would make the cut, but with some careful use of linguistic smoke and mirrors, the fact that I collect and "use" cigars could be softened somewhat. I could always choose to exclude the whole issue entirely, which would require me to leave the "Hobbies and

Interests" section largely blank, as I don't really do anything else (aside from work, write and watch a bit of sport). It's apparently the most challenging part of the vitae to complete. *Folding pillowcases sensitively* comes across as rather weird. I'll just make something up that sounds more interesting and won't engender any unnecessary judgement. I'm aware of someone who once put "Dolphin Handler" on their vitae. It's much easier to sell ourselves by virtue of credible and tangible evidence and experience. But, really, that whole section should just be scrapped – it's basically irrelevant and 99 per cent fabrication.

However, I may be wrong here. Not so much about the fabrication part, but whether or not it is relevant to our vitae, and therefore to each individual creating it. For my part, I am lucky enough to have been blessed thus far with a relatively lengthy career that has spanned a number of high-impact positions across three continents. My education, training and experience is – in my own eyes of course – extensive. As much as my background may allow me to realistically apply for various positions in multiple fields for decent remuneration, I am, in fact, sick and tired of my vitae. Maybe you feel the same way, for different reasons.

For those of you who are "just starting out" (a completely nonsensical phrase for anyone old enough to prepare a vitae, as you clearly "started out" a while ago), your training and experience may very well be limited. As such, your hobbies and interests section may be much more heavily populated to make up for the perceived shortfalls of your more academic credentials. Therefore to you it isn't irrelevant. To others, of course, it might be, which is why we all tend not to be overly selective when we send our vitae out to those looking for it (or not looking for it). We may also have different versions of our vitae to apply for different positions and thereby increase our chances of success.

And we are the same with each other and within our relationships. Just how many versions of you are there? You don't have to answer that question metaphorically (at least not yet), but literally will do for now. You know as well as I do that you have more than one vitae. If you furiously claim that you don't, I would wager a somewhat hefty amount of currency that you would adjust your vitae to enhance your competitiveness for something you really wanted – a new job, a new partner. Your vitae is yours to command, and you would be a dolphin handler if it got you what you wanted. We all have a porpoise in this life. Gates exist for a reason, and I will politely excuse myself safely behind the one that deals with horrendously corny puns. It's the Brit in me – we cannot recuse ourselves from our own nature. But there will come a time for you, for me, for everyone, that too much of one thing reaches saturation point. Our innumerable vitae become as unstable, unsteady and unconvincing as they have always been, especially the older you get.

At my age, at this stage of my life, my creation of multiple editions of me has slowed right down. I am close to consolidating my various vitae into one, that will remain forever as such. We all get to this stage eventually. It's exhausting to be all things to all people. We can also remove half of the stuff that we did, or what we were trained in (i.e. trained "to do"), because it's either out of date, or was never all it was cracked up to be in the first place. We put it there because we thought it mattered, and also put it there because it might matter to someone else. Anything to get that edge. All that training we had no choice but to attend. All of those mandatory courses that enhanced our humanity and made us into such a nice person. All of that learning. And all of it becoming so comparatively, progressively inconsequential as our days lengthen and our eyes lose their youthful shine.

Older people don't just slow down because they get older. They slow down because they come to the realisation they always could, and the things that once made them fret, fuss or fume lose a lot of their bite and bile. They can look at their vitae through a different lens and not really give a hoot about it at all, despite how manicured and magnificent it may look in its almost final, glorious edition. It's not really a paradox, but you can't get to that state of being until you get there. It is not an outcome that can ever be foreshortened. Our eyes may lose their sparkle, but glints of twinkly wisdom manifest themselves instead, even if for the most part we are chuckling quietly to ourselves while simultaneously shredding our vitae to add to recycling.

As such, you can find me on a secluded bench, preferably in the shade of a glorious tree, smoking a fine cigar, sipping happily from a hip flask, and not wishing to be interrupted or annoyed by the flurry of your frenetic, immature existence. Just leave me alone. If you feel like me, your vitae probably looks something like mine. If you don't, then perhaps you are just starting out. I would ask you not to take offence, but someone else already did that for you, whether you like it or not.

# Chapter 7: Discourse

*I waited while you spoke, I listened to your reasoning; while you were searching for words I gave you my full attention.*

*Job 32:11*

Have you ever jumped out of an aeroplane while smoking a cigar? Are you sick and tired of me droning on about these two things? I wouldn't blame you if you were.

Whether you have or you haven't is irrelevant. Neither have any impact on the other whatsoever. I bring up these entirely separate, distinct and unrelated – but inherently risky – activities again, to highlight one of our most favourite pastimes: arguing. And doing it extremely, almost comedically, badly. I include myself fully in this sobering assessment.

We can call it arguing, or debating, or discussing, or having a chat – all modes of discourse – but the manner in which we do all of these things has become rather obvious, at least when it comes to that all-important element of the argument in the first place: *proving our point.* Another way of describing this would be: *getting our point across.* Whether or not we are aware of what our point is supposed to be half the time appears largely extraneous, as we'll typically revert to using the same tactics to "win" the debate irrespective of facts, history, general consensus or anything else that could be construed as meaningfully credible in the alternative to our own point of view.

If I smoked five cigars a day, the likelihood of me dying in a parachute jump would be exactly the same as if I smoked fifty cigars a day. The fact I wouldn't do a parachute jump has nothing whatsoever with my chances of dying in one in relation to my cigar addiction. Accordingly, if I gave up smoking completely, this wouldn't make parachute jumping any safer for me in the slightest. I can't increase my chances of survival by offsetting one risk against the other when they have nothing in common.

If you consider the statistics of dying in a car crash, you have a much higher chance of being involved in a fatal accident while in a car than in a plane. However, if you gave up flying, your chances of dying in a car crash would remain the same. If you also gave up extreme body piercing, skiing, motorbike riding, watching soap operas, social media and Friday night pizza, the risk remains completely unchanged as to whether or not you could die in a road traffic accident, if your driving habits remained the same despite your lack of other apparently risky behaviours. We know these things – we know we can't offset our risks in this way, but we bicker just like we don't. All the time.

The way we manage, manifest and mitigate our own risks is very much akin to the way we argue and try to reason with each other. Here is conflation in its purest, simplest and most bountiful form. It literally and liberally drips from us almost every time we open our big mouths. We have become superlative at it.

Seeing this in its most vainglorious abundance is perhaps no more evident than it is with online comments – there's no slim pickings here. Pick some online rag and peruse an article about politics and politicians, for example, then scroll down to what the people like us have to say. Here is polarisation also at its best, with inconsequential bits of vitae – ours and everyone else's – scattered liberally upon those virtual pages in a condensed attempt to yet again prove our points. It's like shooting fish in a barrel. Only, we're the fish.

If you can't recall the last time you updated your vitae, you have almost assuredly quoted from it in recent weeks, possibly in order to try and settle a debate – in your favour, online or off. It may not have mattered what the debate was all about, but if you felt it wasn't going your way, you could have pulled rank and stated that you were more "qualified" in a particular area (and therefore qualified to win the little argument you were in, or side argument you had created), or you could have demonstrated that your training, education and experience clearly proved that you were right. Even if you were way off the mark. On other occasions you may randomly pull from the vitae of others if it helps prop up your cause. *Well, my best friend is a lawyer and she said. My dad worked for thirty years as an engineer and he said. I read an article and it said.* You could be arguing about bananas and you'll still see and hear these random snippets of inapplicability. We like holding up oranges to prove that bananas exist.

The conflation part is the complete and utter irrelevance of the points we make to try and prove our point, which is the absolute point that our argument itself becomes immediately null and void – i.e. the moment we lose the handle, lose our grip, and, well, just lose the plot completely. If we're in a screaming match with a loved one, have had a bit to drink, and are stressed out beyond all measure of coping, we won't necessarily be quoting from our vitae, but we'll almost certainly be bringing up stuff that is altogether immaterial to the crux of our current crisis. We all do it. We probably always will, but recognising it instantly when we are doing it, and when others are doing it, particularly in the heat of the moment, is possibly not a skill we can acquire without giving up vast, practically incalculable swathes of ground. Being territorial creatures by nature, this is not going to be easy.

It would be a start to at least acknowledge it and take action on it when it happens in writing, but oh so burdensome that has become in itself. There's an awful lot of writing out there – I include these very words – and a lot of it is very awful. I hope to at least exclude the majority of these words from that judgement. When noise has become the norm it is difficult to concentrate, particularly when we are contributing to that noise in the first place.


In the early nineties I was working in a large bookshop in the UK. My little team had a most wonderful manager and she arrived back at our departmental area one day and sat down at her desk, looking at the few of us with a slightly bemused expression. *I'm getting email,* she announced. *All the managers are getting email.*

At that time, I'd never heard of email. None of us really had. We quizzed her for quite some time, trying to establish what on earth she was talking about, and how on earth her computer (which had hitherto only ever been used to check stocked items) could now somehow replace those printed memos to which we were so long accustomed and extremely fond of. We simply could not wrap our heads around it. Nowadays, we appear barely able to survive without it. And we're only talking about a decade, give or take, between my former manager saying those memorable words, and our wholesale, sweeping embrace of this new communication medium – mere milliseconds in human social history. Add another decade or so onto that, and within that time we created and cradled to our chests even more abundant forms of wireless discourse, many of them mere replicas of others, but all of them slightly different enough to warrant our fond, fierce attention and application.

Given that so much of our discourse is now electronic, our conflation skills have had to adapt, and adapt quickly. That part wasn't too difficult. But whereas in physical conversation we have the nuances of body language, body shape and body odour, the virtual realm shields us from our most primitive attributes. We do an awful lot of arguing via computer, and as is probably obvious, we are atrocious at it. Furthermore, the expediency of the medium has in itself become another of our great flawed convergences. The hugely compressed time frame in which we have had to adapt in our social lives, workplaces and institutions to all those forms of electronic conversation has not reflected well on us. It perhaps just isn't natural, or at the very least we are in the early and experimental stages of its evolution, as much as we vainly believe we have a handle on it and consider it as good for us.

Our online communication skills are therefore quite often rubbish, and only ever seem to be desperately trying to catch up. We have on the one hand the most convenient, brilliant and instantaneous ability to communicate with each other, and on the other our never-ceasing ability to communicate badly with each other. We confused the ease of the process with the preciousness of direct human interaction, and have been unable to extrapolate ourselves from the chaos we have since faced – no matter how many new laws we have hastily assembled and enacted to mitigate the online damage, or the policies and procedures we have thrown around like stardust in an attempt to make us all behave and comply with our new electronic tools. We didn't ever play that nicely in the real sandbox.

Email, and associated electronic messaging, has invaded our consciousness in a subtle, divisive, damaging way. There is something about it that by its own instant nature it seems to want to demand from us an instant response, whether we want to or not. As to whether we need to is a whole subsequent chapter, but messages in our "inbox" are hard to ignore – and we have copious inboxes scattered across many of our devices, in most rooms in our homes, and on various parts of our body. They drag us in, and drag us down in ways unimaginable only a short time ago. They are a form of discourse so relatively new and alien to our nature that the insidious effect they are having is slowly devaluing our humanity, gradually dissolving our hardiness, and steadily dismantling our ancient structures before our eyes, beneath our feet, and beyond our comprehension.

Sometimes the straw that breaks the camel's back in any day of our frantic computerized lives is not the troublesome email we get at work, but the kindly message from a loved one. We look at it and panic, as we do not have a moment to respond. Who we have time for, when we are so continually bombarded, is sometimes not them. Neither is it us. We may end up responding, yet not really responding at all, as our response is to say we will respond later. We simply run out of time, and then reset the clock only to run out of time all over again. Our very communication has lost its elemental, visceral purpose, and satisfaction. It has become as meaningless, diluted and tasteless as only we could achieve. We think these tools are doing us good. They are not.

Yet as the saying goes, a bad workman blames his tools. It's not the technology that is slapping us repeatedly about the face as if with a wet kipper, but we do seem to have a proclivity towards being slapped. Many of our greatest inventions over the centuries have been met with extraordinary dismay and sometimes apocalyptic warnings, but we worked it all out in the end some way, somehow. Maybe we will learn to handle our new modes of communication with more dexterity, discretion and dignity than we do at present, or we will face a continued diminishment of the elemental traits that advanced our humanity to begin with. The more plugged in we choose to be, the more plugged up we will become. And we haven't yet invented a tool to clear up that problem.

Communication is one of our most precious resources. For millennia it has been costly and artistic, in every far flung meaning of these descriptors. In a very short space of time, however, it has become nothing more than a chore. And the less we are talking with each other, the less we are truly communicating. Even our conversations, and therefore our arguments, reflect the disjointed, convenient, incoherent and badly-spelled nature of our electronic interchanges. Ironically enough, much of the time we are talking with each other, we're more focused on the electronic devices anyway. Sadly, if skills aren't used, they get lost. Without being a proponent of doom, we are heading inexorably down this path whether care to see it or not. And when we reach the dark, dank, dismal end, we won't be able to talk ourselves out of it, or away from it, as by that time we'll just be stumbling mutely along, our way lit only by the lights of our little screens, perhaps wondering what life was like before such shadow overcame us. Perhaps not.

That's up to us.

# Chapter 8: Nothing



I n a world of instant responses, one such response is to do absolutely nothing. We have trouble with that.

Most of our laws are reactive; many of our policies and procedures are proactive. A law sits there, waiting, not really doing anything until it is called upon to react. Our policies and procedures tend, more often than not, to govern how we should act in the moment – at school, in the workplace and within our institutions – not necessarily what could happen to us when we don't. That's largely the domain of the law.

It is illegal to commit murder, burgle someone's home, or rob them in them the street. The vast majority of us don't do these things because they are illegal – we don't do them because we have a moral framework and those things are, as is hopefully evident, wholeheartedly, unequivocally wrong. It's not as if we need the law to tell us that they are wrong – we need it to kick into action when such wrongs happen and ensure that the perpetrator receives the appropriate sanction. The law is nothing more than this, and never has been. It is not a behavioural guide. It does not recommend how you should act. The law cannot make you do anything when you are not doing it. Nor can it stop you from doing something. It is there just in case you do.

We have had to create a lot of new laws to cope with the demands and complexities of our modern existence. As contemplated in the previous chapter, our online world has spawned a plethora of legislation to deal with misbehaviour in the virtual realm, and along with this a host of associated documents, consults, guides, policies and procedural mapping now exist in our own daily lives, wherever we may find ourselves. At a former workplace of mine there was a faded sheet of paper pinned to a much-abandoned noticeboard explaining how to use a computer mouse. It was there from 1996 to 2018, and is probably still hanging around. We've had to pin up other such explanations in even more recent times — not so much to deal with the mechanics of our equipment, but the malevolence of our behaviours. We've gone from: *here's how to use this thing,* to: *here's how to use it nicely.* Perhaps we never anticipated having to do the latter quite as much as we do.

It is in light of the latter that we have felt the need to come up with these various laws to deal with our bad behaviour in general. We have introduced enhanced pieces of legislation to react to public disorder, racist incidents, causing offence, bullying, harassment and discrimination — online, or off. As considered in an earlier chapter, some of our defining (or redefining) laws set a new precedent where perception now plays a pivotal role at the outset. In such instances, the law has no choice but to react. We have forced its hand. We did not give ourselves the opportunity to do nothing.

Quite a number of years ago, but well within the kind of time frame referred to above, a former colleague of mine stated that since mobile phones started to become more widespread, calls to the police – for trivial matters – increased exponentially. And as those new electronic modes of discourse flourished, so did the trivia. The best of human advancement was being matched by the worst of human conduct and lack of moral fortitude. And, as is rather apparent, we gave ourselves little option but to respond to each report of nonsense. We set fickleness, flummery and frivolity upon new thrones and have been bowing to their commands ever since.

In a not so far off world where human communication options consisted of talking person to person, writing a letter, using a telephone or sending a fax (which is pretty much what I grew up with), the idea of reporting something frivolous to the authorities wasn't much within our mindset, not that we weren't annoyed by the same kinds of things as we are today. We just had less electronic noise in our lives and way fewer laws telling us we were victims even if we weren't. We wouldn't have considered making a special trip to our local police station (and here, "police station" can also be a metaphor) to say that we'd been upset by a nasty, harassing glance from our neighbour, and wanted something done about it. Nowadays, the police have databases swamped with reported incidents and "crimes" as insipid as this. Yet we have continued to encourage each other, and ourselves, to believe that doing nothing is no longer at our discretion, even when faced with utter inanity. We've always been bad enough at dealing with each other (neighbourly disputes are an ancient affair), but our present, nannying environment provides limited option to shake our heads and walk away without some kind of reference number being automatically generated, and a host of policies waiting to make everything and everyone better. How nice.

And as this state of affairs has cemented itself within our mental, moral and institutional frameworks, we have reached a stage where it is almost impossible not to react, in nearly all contexts. And we fully expect and vociferously demand those reactions – a non-response is unacceptable. Even our electronic communications have built-in functionality to show that our message (i.e. gripe) has been delivered. Then it sits there in someone else's inbox. And we sit there, drumming our fingers on the table, waiting for our deserved acknowledgement and action. The longer we have to wait, even if it's only been ten minutes, the more annoyed we get. *They've seen my message, why haven't they responded? Why? I'm going to send another one and complain.* We wouldn't cope very well if we had to go back to the days of the telegram. And the person to whom our message has been sent knows they have to respond, and their messages are building up, and the policies and procedures are clear: do something. Do something *now*.

We have created a system, for want of a better word, that is systematically, frantically and unsuccessfully being designed, redesigned and overhauled to cope with the fragmenting and fraying edges of our social construct. This breakdown is happening now in real time more often than not. The more we disintegrate, the more safety nets we need to create to catch the falling, broken pieces. Each net is a new piece of legislation or policy, and if someone shrieks loud enough that they need their own special safety net, we tend to give it to them. We've been handing out nets like candy to the screaming child for years, and still they want more. They are not sated, neither are they satisfied, and they'll create more problems and demand more nets for things that should never have been considered as "issues" in all of our wildest, weirdest imaginings. Our lack of ability to say: *no, this is not an issue* is no longer a thing. Their things are things now, and it appears there's nothing we can do about it. We let this happen. This is on us.

It would be an interesting – if not nigh on impossible task – to create a procedural document that stipulated all of those times where doing nothing was appropriate, especially due to the current conditions we find ourselves in. We do have a few guidelines in place, particularly in our workplaces, to deal with this issue in some respects, but we have to suffer some extreme behaviours first. If you work in an environment that administers or oversees in any way the lives and livelihoods of people, there exist those regulars. You know who they are. They're the ones bombarding the call centre daily, or your inbox daily, or testing your voicemail system capacity to the limit daily, and their communications are either abusive, obnoxious, erroneous, inappropriate or simply off the wall. They have been provided with multiple responses – most of them the same, but in the end the policy manual states that "noting their concerns on their file" is an appropriate response in itself, if all other avenues have been exhausted. It's still a response – it's not nothing – but it's about the closest we usually get to doing nothing. Everything else is a whole load of something.

For the mainstream, however, we will also have in our heads that our concerns are warranted and legitimate, even though we would not necessarily behave like a "regular", and we are now just as conditioned into thinking that answers are always required, and fast. Whether we are sending or receiving those messages – and our work and personal lives demand both in comparable measure sometimes – we struggle to step down, step back, and step away, without doing a thing.

There are much wider implications to this widespread turn of events in our social and employment lives. An expectation of a decisive response to any particular grievance – perceived or otherwise – is evident everywhere we look, particularly in our online realm. *Why don't they do something about that? They should do something about that. Something needs to be done about that.* On a grand scale, our demand for action has become much more prominent and far-reaching, and it's not difficult to find trouble (of our own making) when we are constantly looking for it. We even have our celebrities waiting in the wings to take up any cause or jump on any bandwagon to carry the momentum forwards. Some of these personalities by virtue of how they look, where they came from, how they dress, or simply what opinion they decide to express on any given day can transform them immediately into a global ambassador for change. The difference nowadays between celebrities and politicians also appears rather negligible.

As noted in the previous chapter, the extraordinary pace of change within a very compressed time frame regarding our modes of electronic communication may not be, or may not have been, all that good for us, as much as we have seemingly embraced it all without compunction. There is no frame of reference anywhere in our history where such swift, all-encompassing, radical, earth-shattering change was a positive thing for any society. We have simply not caught up with what happened, and what is still happening, but we are using tools of enormous power as if they are toys. And we are flinging toys out of our strollers at every chance we get regarding issues of staggering complexity and often global significance. A mere tantrum can start a war. Not that this is new, but everyone can see it happening now in real time. And we can all join in with the flurry and the fury, pointing out what we want, how we want, when we want, and everyone can see what is making us so mad. Our own grievances, or standing up for the cause of others, has an instant, enraptured audience across the world.

If the grievance was highlighting something systemic dis-covered in an institution, for example, the response is hasty and universally guaranteed. Victim groups are interviewed. Celebrities gather and gush. The hearths of outrage are fuelled and lit. Crowds assemble. Politicians trip over each other, and over their words: promising, placating, pledging instant transformation. It is taken seriously. Heads will roll. Training will be rolled out. Changes will be made. We will not accept this kind of behaviour within our organisations or from any individual. Commentators and comedians alike jab and swipe and spit. Pitchforks appear on the horizon. Martyrs and murals are made. Social media melts down, again. Context gets a little hazy.

Yet doing nothing here is not an option, nor should it be. The more we look for systemic problems, the more we will find. It's probably why they're called "systemic" to begin with. It's what we do. We have no idea how many ugly problems we may have thwarted from becoming systemic over the years, but we can always identify the ones that got away and got really bad over time. Seek and ye shall find, and when we find them, we can be shaken to our very core. For we seem almost surprised sometimes when an evil has been discovered, often one that has festered for decades, with what seems like oblivion, incompetence or wilful complicity in keeping it hidden. We shouldn't be at all surprised, however, and we should without question make every effort to deal with it – at all levels.

Our apparent astonishment is sad evidence of our collective lack of humility, and represents a vain belief we should have already arrived at our utopia by now, and everyone should help that happen. This in turn creates a sense of social shame that magnifies our hysteria even more. And increased shame amplifies blame. Back to our online soap boxes.

For accompanying our quest to root out these evils nowadays is an overwhelming desire to ensure that such malfeasance is somehow representative of everyone, everywhere. This desire tends to emanate from the fringes, but the fringe gets a lot of air time and makes a lot of noise, as we are all too aware. If one hospital has a few staff members found to be making racial slurs, for example, suddenly the whole of the health authority has systemic racist problems. If one police officer does something heinous, the whole world goes up in flames. Where the pendulum may once have swung to downplay, downgrade or downright deny such behaviours, it has lurched vigorously into the realms of zealotry, fanaticism and revenge. All forms of moderation are lost.

A terrible side effect of finding out just how nasty we have been, and how extremely nasty we can be, results in extreme responses where we try to tear down the whole structure, rather than take it back to the studs. That wrecking-ball response demanded by the rioters and those extremists of political and moral thought has gained sufficient traction, and the momentum has shifted universally towards wholesale, sweeping, immediate and irrevocable changes. Yet dismantling the entire framework will only result in replacing it with something just as bad – we cannot recuse ourselves from our own nature. There are only so many ideologies to go round, and they will continue to go round. We are the problem here, and will remain ever so.

Our institutions only mirror who we are and what we want. If we end one, we'll only start another. Order is replaced with order. Ending one routine is never the end of routine, even terrible and terrifying ones. Pulling down a statue leaves a void as large, as obvious and as painful as the monument itself.

So in plain sight of all these extremes – be it the neighbour who has taken umbrage at a mere glance and now clutches their very own special crime reference number, the regular caller yelling at the call centre staff, the hard Left propagandist demanding the dismantling of an institution, the hard Right agitator raising a hand to brute control, and all the noise, fuss, disorder and chaos accompanying them – how could we now operate with the option of doing nothing as an option itself? We've created a monster, but at the same time it took this approach to identify other monsters. Part of our problem is that we don't know when to put our foot on the brake, and some people need to simply pipe down. Celebrities in particular.

So perhaps we don't need to worry too much about the fact we have been forced to abandon doing nothing as an option, as the nuances of non-response are so specific, so case sensitive, that you can't – and never really could – convert them into anything resembling a coherent or suitable procedure to begin with. The wider social damage has been done, and it appears irreversible, but hope remains. It's therefore not so much that we should do *nothing* – more like do nothing crazy, nothing extreme. Light emerges from its source. Let the middle illuminate the edges. We have to work reasonably with what we have, and who we have, and if we can realise that we are the cause and not the solution to most of the problems we are so keen to identify – particularly in others, and in our institutions – then sometimes we won't have to necessarily "do" anything, which is in some respects the most powerful way of simply doing nothing.

# Chapter 9: Plan



*If you play the fool and exalt yourself, or if you plan evil, clap your hand over your mouth!*

*Proverbs 30:32*

Have you got a plan? Have I got a plan? I guess we'll find out one way or another.

In my years of conscious presence on this furiously rotating globe that we call home, I have yet to encounter a question quite so precise, incisive and demanding as *have you got a plan?* It cuts through the fat and the gristle to get to the meat in a way that other simple queries can't quite manage. It isn't the only prescient question of self-direction out there, but for me it rates high on a list of things I should probably enquire of myself more often than not, and I would do well to try and answer said question whenever I feel resolute enough to ask it. In doing so I may very well help to avoid some ridiculously bad decision-making and set my feet upon a more enlightened path, even if that light only gets me a few more minutes or hours along my journey without falling down a pit, before the shadows lengthen, and the darkness plays its inevitable hand. Claiming to see too far ahead is as dubious as most weather forecasts, so for the most part this should be a daily thing, if not multiple times a day. Most religions would suggest an ongoing (perhaps altogether wholesale) commitment to such circumspect devotion, and there's maybe a point there, somewhere.

Having a plan, however, isn't always about creating a schedule and sticking it on the fridge. The question can be far more ethereal than this, and our responses are not necessarily ones we could write down, or would even want to. When you start scraping the bottom of the barrel of your own soul, the sludge isn't exactly pretty. Not the kind of selfie that makes the cut. *Here's the feculent scum of my selfish, obnoxious, unkind, lying, cheating, puny existence. Fancy a date?* We don't really have a plan at all, do we. But we are most worthy bedfellows of each other, which is why relationships remain a thing, and always will. We haven't had too much trouble creating, recreating and procreating the best and the very worst of us.

It's quite challenging to find a plan in the heat of the moment. If you're in that yelling match with a loved one *(How can you have a gate there? How can you not have a gate there? Etc.)* and you try to psych them out by asking if they have a plan, it may backfire abruptly. They may reach for the nearest robust object to clunk you over the head with, which constitutes a plan, and I can't say a bad one: that bruise would be well deserved. A skull fracture not so much, but fights can always escalate far beyond what we would ever imagine happening sometimes – we are creatures of emotion after all. It may be a slightly safer option for you to step back, count slowly to a suitable two digit number, and state quite firmly that *you* don't have a plan, and that you are sorry.

Yes, we're all going to be doing this in every single argument from now on. I'm sure this sermon is going down well. Try having a glass or two of wine and practising the formula in front of the mirror by yourself. Possibly better to know how it feels when you're in the state that you do most of your regular squabbling anyway. Much better than taking a vain selfie. (Remember not to play the fool and exalt yourself.) If you're teetotal, you shouldn't have any problem whatsoever in getting it right first time in your very next clash.

Then there are those times where we need to clap our hand over our mouth, particularly if we are planning evil. As far as self-assessment goes, I believe the hand to mouth gesture is a realisation that the plan is bad, and that we should stop. Evil people don't tend to do this, clearly, and their plans succeed. So if you don't consider yourself a heinous, malevolent, destructive person hell-bent on havoc, I would expect your hand to be in front of your mouth more often than not, perhaps stifling the gasp of horror at the comprehension of just how stupid or damaging your plan really was before you went ahead and enacted it. We don't have to be evil in the most antiquated definition of the word for our plans to cause untold chaos, even ones that appeared all nice and shiny when we dreamt them up. It's not really about coming up with "good" plans, more like ones that aren't so bad. The phrase *sounds like a plan* is as kindly ambiguous and genuinely respectful to our proclivities as it may appear. *That's a really good idea* generally isn't. Only dictators, autocrats, narcissists and persons of such ilk need to hear this kind of praise.

We need to be a bit more discerning, and a little less stuck up. Let's call that place the middle.

We cannot avoid plans, wherever we may find ourselves –

particularly the plans of others. If your workplace is one that manages the health, education, welfare, financial issues, legal issues, safety issues, personal issues, behavioural issues, and all other manner of issues related to the everyday calamity and collapse of the human condition, you will no doubt be formulating many plans on a daily basis, some within extremely tight and stressful deadlines. Case plans, health plans, surgery plans, service plans, education plans, harm reduction plans, safety plans, financial plans – lots and lots of planning. Some of these plans need to change rapidly, and many are simply constructed on the fly. Emergency response involves plans flying over the airwaves as fast as the vehicles flying to the scene of the problem, with even more hastily assembled plans by the persons responsible for arriving there, when they get there. If there's violence, weapons, or agitation beyond measure, all planning can go out of the window. At that stage it's just purely damage limitation – that is typically the plan in its entirety.

The front line is really a series of lines, or we can also liken them to waves. Imagine a pebble thrown into a pond, and the waves rippling outwards. The first ripple is the baton charge – the first responders. Paramedics, police, fire service, social workers, and all manner of emergency services whose remit and role it is to turn up at the chaos before everyone else. Close behind these are the second ripple – still very much a front line, but picking up the pieces directly afterwards and dealing with the wider side effects created by the initial incident. Imagine a policing unit tasked with attending a violent domestic dispute. A suspect is arrested and a victim identified. Now that the immediate threat of violence has in some measure been curtailed, there kicks into action a second wave of persons involved – custodians, specialised crime divisions, witness interviewers – all following some kind of plan, and all very much front facing.

As the process moves through the system, and the latter ripples extend outwards, even more background services are called upon. One pebble can create a lot of waves, and a heck of a lot of subsequent planning. Yet it's often a lot safer to plan when you are several ripples behind the earlier ones. It doesn't necessarily make it easier, and your role may be extraordinarily stressful, but you are not facing down that urgent, ugly, unsightly chaos at the very heat of the moment that initiated your current workload. You have a bit more time to plan, and a lot more time to blame the actions of those who rippled out far ahead of you towards the bedlam in the first place. By the time it gets to you, and the plans (i.e. decisions) of others have also filtered their way through to you in various forms – emails, notes, reports, in-person discussions, you know that you are going to have to create a whole new plan, or set of plans, some of which are to mitigate the plans others made in the first place – even those who are on your "team". *What on earth where they thinking? How could they not have a gate there? Wow, that was dumb.*

Of course, the ripples don't end there. The front line doesn't get the full brunt of the blame, even though they are the ones most likely to have videos of them uploaded to social media – just ask Matt. As things move forwards, those folks picking up the pieces of others will also make plans later held brutally to account, and on it goes, and on and on. Pebble after pebble, wave after wave, usually overlapping. The waters are never calm, never still. Multiply this by countless millions and millions of issues, daily, nightly, across every boundary, borderline and barrier, and there we are. That's our society. Welcome to the plan. And where are you in all of this mess?

Our plan, their plan, your plan, my plan. Have we got a plan? It's all about decision-making, and that's where it is always easier to stand on the sidelines and scream at the decisions made by others. So what's your plan? Either stand in the middle, plug the gap, and expose yourself to scrutiny every day, every waking moment, or hide at the fringes, in the shadows, and vociferously appear when it suits you best. For if that's your plan, you'd better clap that hand of yours to your mouth sooner rather than later, or you are little more than a pebble.

Which takes us back to the soul sludge. Depending on the murkiness of your intangible self, you may find yourself on any given day, or moment, being much more of a pebble than you planned to be. We all create ripples, waves, and chaos. Some of us, perhaps without ever really knowing why, are constantly flinging ourselves into the calm waters of others (waters that they are trying their hardest to keep calm, which is in itself a very trying thing to do), generating wave after wave, and disturbing the stillness that they are so desperate to be in the presence of. Some of us are flung there by others, without our knowledge or consent, and find ourselves used and abused in ways we would, or could, never plan to happen, let alone ever want to imagine.

At any point in time we are a pebble or a ripple – we are the cause of the problem, or doing something a result of it, whether we like it or not. Those ripples are inevitable. Some of us are the first wave, heading uncertainly into uncertainty. Chaos doesn't reveal its full hand to us just because it knows we're on the way; and our waves break upon it, often with tragic consequences. Some of us are blissfully unaware that our choices, decisions and actions – all of which are the sum of our plans – are a daily pebble, or a number of pebbles, for a lot of people. As someone once told me of a client of hers: *he has no idea just how much work he really is.* Still others simply don't care either way.

In the midst of all we do for people in our work lives, our home lives, and our social lives, there exist our own plans. Short-term, mid-term, long-term. We think we can see the light at the end of the tunnel, sometimes, but like those dreams where our legs feel leaden, and we are wading as if through a swamp, getting towards that light is no mean feat. Yet that's the plan, and we push towards it, making things up as we go along. None of us are experts in getting there, as much as others may think they are.

And the plans we have, like our vitae, tend to consolidate as our years go by, and the tunnel is longer behind us as it is before us. Our plans unfold, become more straightforward, with less at stake and less scrutiny. We can somewhat step back from the pebbles and the ripples, now choosing to be neither, with our plans so simple, so ordered, so innocuous, that we have the opportunity to explore and enjoy our safe harbour, without the burden of other people's complications disrupting our peace and calm waters. Perhaps that's what being "old" is supposed to be like.

But that's maybe just a pipe dream. Retirement is generally our favourite plan – the light we are most focused on – but for many of us it turns into chaos, even if we were lucky enough to get there in the first place. For some, their tunnels collapse around them, blocking out all light, all hope, and all intentions along with it.

Holding out for utopia is our best, and worst, of plans.

# Chapter 10: Side

*The people of the city were divided; some sided with the Jews, others with the apostles.*

*Acts 14:4*

We have been picking sides for a very long time. It's what we do. Even watching a sport game that we have no particular interest in whatsoever (e.g. neither of the teams are "ours") we will still pick a side. We simply can't help it. Staying neutral involves a lot more effort than we realise. Probably as there's really no such thing. Most of our Super Bowl parties consist almost exclusively of cheering spectators who have waged a bet on one team, and they want them to win because of the cash prize, not because they ever wanted them to win in the first place. If we can't get what we want from our own side, we'll find some temporary satisfaction in another.

People also want us to pick sides because they already have, or feel that they need to, and quickly. And our choices are often quite limited – it's one, or the other. Decision-making is typically a two-dimensional process. This is probably the most distilled down description of democracy I can come up with.

If we have chosen a side, we expose ourselves to scrutiny from the other. It goes with the territory. And with those powerful tools of ours so readily available at our fingertips, we can face the relentless, excessive venting of our opposition 24/7. Even if we wake up at midnight, there's no stopping it. We are all immediately and irrevocably connected now, and there's no going back. I say "connected". That's not true at all. We are completely and utterly disconnected.

When picking a side, we have a variety of options at our disposal. If we choose to do some research, for example, we may find that one particular tablet software system appeals to us more than the other. Using the reviews and recommendations of others, and our own instincts, we make our decision and are possibly ultimately satisfied. Or, we buy both and save ourselves the hassle of having to decide in the first place. This is more difficult when it comes to picking who we "choose" to lead us. The criteria are rather more ambiguous to say the least.

For the most part, in our democratic institutions, the choice is often one or the other. Regardless of whether or not we had the opportunity of picking from several, it often comes down to eliminating the extras, and choosing between the remaining two. We are hardwired to pick sides this way. Yet when there's only two to begin with, as is often the case, we've already made our decision before we've made it, and that's exactly what our opposition hates the most. *How can you have a gate there? How can you not have a gate there?* Welcome to the political spectrum. It's not much of a spectrum if we're honest. Polarisation isn't new. It's just incessantly in our faces and more obvious now than it ever was – to the point where it is the norm – and it amplifies our collective anxiety to the point of squealing, screeching, screaming breakdown.

Have you ever tried to go out and about and leave your mobile phone at home? Have you tried to recuse yourself from all this noise, all this side-picking, side-splitting chaos? It doesn't work, does it. That two week vacation you were so looking forward to (whether you have mobile phone reception or not when there) refreshes and relaxes you, and then you come back to an exploding inbox, and your happiness and peace evaporates in an instant. Our search for utopia is boundless yet always leaves us broken. That's the problem with utopia – it isn't.

The most ferociously vociferous of us – in whatever realm – are the ones most aggressively confident that their side is the one to be on. The more entrenched our position, however, the more static our arguments become. If we aren't gaining enough ground, we'll fire more mortar shells until we think we can, or send willing volunteers across the front line to further our cause, and that's not a tactic that typically works out well – for the "volunteers" at any rate. Mortar shells don't gain ground either just because we've fired them off – that's not their primary purpose. This is about the most distilled down analogy of social or political polarisation I can come up with. When the smoke clears, if it ever does, both sides are exactly where they always were, and the casualties are devastating on either side of the battlefield. What lies between is a scorched wasteland.

While I was studying for my Advanced Level examinations (politely known as A-Levels), albeit the full descriptor may sound more exciting on one's vitae, a 2 year old boy was abducted, tortured and murdered by two 10 year old boys. It was as sudden and calamitous as that. I would not wish to play down in any respect the unadulterated evil of that crime – if that word even comes close – and the shock waves of what happened have reverberated throughout the halls of our collective conscious ever since, even if we'd never heard about it before. We are our history. Our guilt and shame are both always nipping at our heels.

One of my A-Level examinations was in the relatively novel area of Media Studies. When such media was limited to the TV and printed news (and all varieties therein) it did not stop the mutual gasp of horror and revulsion, and unified soul-searching that transpired in the wake of the murder. You didn't need any kind of "social" media to fuel those fires. The nation was in tatters and wanted direction. They used to drop pamphlets out of planes for that very same effect. Put that on your vitae.

We searched frantically for answers. In the absence of online opinion, all opinions were still making their way to the inboxes we had at that time, as slow and cumbersome as they may appear to us now. In the hushed counsel of my classroom there was talk that the incident may form part of our final examination the following year. For word was spreading that the two young child murderers had been watching a particularly violent, degrading film – one that may have implicitly (or explicitly, depending on how you argued it) inspired their heinous actions. This was extraordinary, revelatory, and worthy of the traction it gained. Media Studies had never been so prescient. Our teacher, ever the grave advisor, warned us to be prepared: the question was coming. And she was right.

The following year, even as the national angst was still fully elevated, and answers were being sought at every level as to how this most egregious crime could ever have occurred in the first place, there I was in my late teens being asked to determine whether or not a particular film was pivotal in the brutal murder of a toddler. At least that's how I interpreted it at the time. After all, I was young.

I don't remember the exam itself, or the room I sat in to write it. Couldn't tell you anything about the question, only that it was in the paper. My own youthful anxieties, personal or otherwise, transcended that particular test, but one thing that remains seared into my skull was the abject terror of picking the wrong side. Do I imply that the film was instrumental in the killing, or do I downplay it as irrelevant? What does the examiner want to hear? What do I even know when I am merely a child myself? I didn't ask the last question, but I was certainly fretting over the former ones.

Maybe now that I am a touch older than I was then, or because I have some small appreciation for grading criteria (at least as they were then), I realise that my fear of picking of a side for that particular question was irrelevant. I don't even know how I felt about it at the time, even though I probably made some kind of stand. For they weren't asking me to pick a side. They were asking me to come up with a cohesive, reasonable argument to prove my case, and that was what I was being graded on. Whatever case I had, or thought I had, was immaterial to the question. And oh so erroneous does that sound. Nowadays we are judged not so much on the way we argue a point, but the side we appear to take – irrespective of everything. And everything means everything, particularly context.

You can't debate with a screamer, regardless of which side of the political spectrum they claim to inhabit, or in which vault or veneration of the moral one they aspire to dwell. We can try, but we will fail. Which begs the question, should we even try? And this is where society meets its vanishing point. Send in the pacifiers or send in the army – we seem to be stuck between these extremes, and we have no one but ourselves to blame. We're not quite at the latter yet, but we can get there whenever we want. Maybe as you read these very words we got there, but I sincerely hope that we didn't vanish as expediently as that.

The middle ground is really quite boring. Not a lot happens there, at least not in any hurry. Things carry on as they always have done – in the assumption that they are generally decent and benevolent – and we can all go about our business without fear, fuss or fright. Like a pair of plain, sensible shoes, the middle ground plods along, resisting unnecessary change and grudgingly, if not generously, accepting new ways of doing things. We embrace new modes and methods if we see their purpose, and if they don't shatter our gates. Over time we will accept that some gates should be opened up, and that is good for all concerned. Try to force them open without a plan and we will resist.

The middle doesn't worry too much about picking a side, as we always felt we landed quite naturally on either side of the fence, and certainly close enough to touch it. We are quite content with the central parameters of our position and the general absence of disarray. It's not that we are neutral – quite the contrary – more like a bit of one side, or another. Political debate (or any debate), when we're not so far apart, can be fun – and productive. It's not as if either side of the house will accept that statement in the heat of discussion, but it is evident when we all go home and stop acting the part that we might agree with this in private, occasionally. A healthy opposition is essential to any kind of two-dimensional democratic process, yet the health of our democracy nowadays is severely strained by the dimensions our people and processes inhabit. They are way out there, wherever "there" can accurately be quantified. It certainly doesn't seem grounded in any credible meaning of the word, and they can't even see the fence, let alone who may be standing beside it.

Debate, of all kinds, flourished during the Age of Enlightenment. Now, we've largely switched off all the lights and you can find us in the shadows, our chins barely illuminated by the light of our mobile phones, furiously typing away on our tiny screens and co-operating in the chaos. We have truly forgotten how to discuss an issue without reverting to the same tired, clichéd behaviour – bad temper, bad tactics, bad fruit. We are so paranoid about the side we think we have to take that we don't even bother with the coherent, reasoned argument any longer, as there's no one around to listen to it. We feel the need to match the rantings and ramblings of our opposition with the same level of bewailing and babbling, to the point that everyone who used to be in the middle has packed up and vacated. They're still around – just sick and tired of the mortar shells, and under cover elsewhere. Their voices can still be heard, too, but you have to make a special effort to seek them out.

It's not about what side you are on, or think you're on. Can you touch the fence? Can you even see the fence? If so, you are getting close. It's the only frame of reference that matters. Once you can reach out a hand of yours – presumably the one not clutching your device – and touch that ancient structure, and feel the firm, old, implacable material from which it is formed, you may breathe some small sigh of relief. Your heart rate may slow down ever so slightly and your ears relax a bit without the incessant buzzing to which they are so long accustomed. You may even realise that you didn't need to pick a side, as you've found yourself right where you should be, whichever side it is.

That's the quiet, assuaging power of the middle.  It is only there can we find our true definition.

99

# Chapter 11: Kind



*1 Corinthians 13:4*

Of all the things that love is, the above statement is not exhaustive. More like exhausting. For patience and kindness alone take a lot out of us, particularly when we are personally or professionally obligated to exhibit such glorious traits in the face of opposing, antagonistic behaviours. Our workplace policies and procedures don't tend to quote Bible verses, but the basic structure – and intent – of verses such as this have transposed themselves onto the fabric of our existence whether we like it or not. I would hope, however, that being patient and kind would make it on to the top of most of our lists of worthy virtues anyway, and accordingly find their way woven into our everyday behaviours, albeit phrased somewhat less directly, and possibly trying not to sound too "religious" or imposing at the same time. After all, we do not want to offend people by being completely inoffensive to begin with.

The word "kind" derives from the word "kin". And when it comes to kindness, the kin part is relevant. There is an innateness infused into the word at its most elemental level, where all definitions of it don't do justice to how the word *felt* over time to the particular kin exhibiting its qualities, not what it meant purely in technical terms for the purposes of dictionary definitions. Certainly not our fake and fluffy understanding of the word nowadays. That innateness is that of character, of form, of order, of condition, of situation. We are akin to our kin in more ways than you could shake a stick at. Our own sense of kindness – and the way we express it – is hardwired into the essence of who we are. The only way we can stop being kind in the particular way that we are kind is to die, or be killed. And the latter would certainly not be very kind.

When we ask our children if they have been kind, we hope that they will know what we mean. We don't ask them if they've "done kind". They don't have to say what they didn't do, but the "being" kind part for a child is very much not doing anything unkind, in the way that they understand it in their developing moral construct. We hope that they will avoid the unkindness parts and, over time, develop a character that is as innately kind as we are. Wherein lies the fatal flaw, but we're not teaching our children to be perfect, after all.

You can't describe kindness very well. Any modern definition doesn't suggest that it is an act of doing, more like a series of agreeable character traits that may lend itself to being a pleasant person to be around. It would be easier to couch it in terms of doing stuff, but it really is an act of being, hence our general inability to easily define what kindness means in general terms. That's probably because it was never supposed to be a general word and applied in a generic manner. If it started with kin, it applies to kin. And kin alone.

If our sense of kinship – our very identity – is damaged, debilitated or destroyed, our kindness takes a battering as well.

That's because they're the same thing. If you tell me to reject my background, my so-named privilege, my innate form (because you hate and despise all of these things), how do you expect a kind response? In fact, how do you expect any response that will do any of us any good? Accordingly, if you have decided for yourself that your own construct should be denied, dismantled or dismissed, you will also not be kind, and your actions will be unkind. But that's OK for you. Just cover it all up with that new one-size-fits-all righteousness you invented and all will be well. If people resist, shout them down, and come up with laws, policies and procedures that stifle their cries even more. And then the opposite side reacts with extreme unkindness – in some respects they had no choice, even though they chose to react that way – and we find ourselves where we are. If kind is high on the list of what love is, I guess that means we're largely being the opposite. And I don't think the antonyms of love make for particularly pleasant reading.

Destroying frameworks as a hallmark of the hard Left (and the hard Right may seek to destroy the people who destroyed their frameworks) results in an awful lot of pain, loss, confusion and unkindness within every group, class, culture, country – whatever word fits: the words that demarcate and describe us according to our kin, even though such statements may be screamed down as racist.

If love = kind, then kinship can be an eternally beneficial, benevolent and beautiful thing. And within that kinship we have been provided the tools and teaching to keep us on the straight and narrow, so that love flourishes – including the kind of love that keeps things generational. Wink, wink. The partial verse quoted at the top of this chapter was written a couple of millennia ago to a particular group of people who, the writer evidently thought, needed more of that straight and narrow. Perhaps not narrow-minded, but at least in clear sight of the fence.

You don't choose to be kin, but you can become kin. It's a process and every group has a different approach (including wholesale takeover), and there are multifarious forms of this process scattered across the world, and throughout history. Some groups do not allow outsiders under any circumstances – their kinship so heavily guarded and protected that it cuts them off. We all know that this doesn't work out very well in the end.

But, accordingly, you can't fabricate or manufacture kinship. It is an organic process. You can't make up processes on behalf of other groups so that you, or anyone else, can "fit in". They'll either have you or not, and that is as much down to them as it is to you to want to fit in, not fit in because you think you deserve to, or because their group should not discriminate against you "just because". Talk to Matt. If you don't know what their "because" is, you probably shouldn't want to be part of their group to begin with. They are allowed their "because" – it's an ancient gate to prevent people like you from busting it open without any coherent reasons whatsoever. Unicorns don't get to go where they want just because they are unicorns.

Integration as a social engineering product isn't very kind, even though it's marketed as the most wonderful, beneficial thing in the universe. Those who have had their gates smashed would appreciate this statement, with a sad irony evident that the ones being encouraged to integrate are very rarely discouraged from smashing any of their own. They can keep them all, because that's diversity in action. We welcome everyone as-is, because we are so incredibly kind. And so incredibly off course. Welcome to our globalised, fractured societies. We impaled ourselves on our own unicorn horn.

Seeing as we are all now playing in this sandbox whether we like it or not, do we have the opportunity to play nicely, or even kindly? The nice part can be forced. Kindness can't. Nice and kind are two opposite ends of a very long stick. We've very much focused on the being nice part because it's easier to implement and conveniently neglects to acknowledge the lack of kindness inherent therein, even though we think nice and kind are the same thing. Welcome back to conflation – we're very fond of this indeed.

We can all be nice, especially when we want to be, or have to be. In our heads, of course, we are muttering unkind things. It's a good thing that thought control isn't a thing yet (it isn't, is it?) as there we'll find enough systemic issues to melt down the entire world, let alone social media. I can see you sitting there in that training session, grimacing internally yet smiling externally, as you are told – yet again – how to behave, how to think, how to get along. How, in essence, this great and glorious plan of ours is working and how you are an integral part of it. Sitting there in silent agony as more of your gates are flung open, as the trainer smiles and you smile nicely back, and she kindly points out all those words you are no longer allowed to say as they are not kind. The more integrated we've become, the less kind we have had to be – in its real meaning. We had to create a new kindness with its own language instead so we can all play nicely in that sandbox. Our new morality can be very hard to stomach sometimes, but still we smile. How nice we are.

And over the years we have endured this state of affairs,

many of us have slowly come to accept that it is the way it is, particularly those of us in the disenfranchised middle, on either close side of that fence. The gateless Leftist utopian vision is nothing new and it is now all pervasive in our societies, in turn creating an equal and possibly opposite set of ugly reactions. However, a lack of voice at the middle is not a lack of disagreement – we were silenced; we did not choose to be so. Not that we were particularly noisy to begin with, which is probably why we would not class ourselves as a screamer, or take ourselves down that path no matter how abject our fear at the current climate. We are very partial to our fence and our kin on both close sides of it. Together we know that between us we can keep things moving forwards at a steady, reasonable, responsible pace. That's what robust, healthy bi-partisan banter is for. It is one of the foundation stones of democracy and reflects ancient kinship in ways we could not ever fully comprehend, but we feel it deeply. We always have and always will. Without that banter, that back-and-forth across the fence, we have nothing more than autocracy, and this has never been kind to us – clearly – for it is not what kinship was meant to be.

It has been more than evident in relatively recent times that we are being encouraged to abandon our individual kinship in favour of the "new" purpose. Any descriptor that does not fit in with our holy social order is rejected without compunction. Whole swathes of us have been castigated as racist. National identities have been scorned, discouraged and disallowed. You are no longer permitted to be who you are. Whatever flag you once flew must now be folded up, if not burned. Might as well burn those books of yours as well – they are no longer required. Learning is over. Leave behind your class, your kin, your clan, your group and institution. You don't need them and they don't need you. This is the amalgamation of us all. It's our new unity, our shared objective. So don't hold on to those individual, old-fashioned, outmoded notions. The gates are open and the vision is clear. You have arrived at the mighty plain; the plan of all plans. Your singularity of purpose is righteous and no one will stand in your way. You will have your tower. So grab a bucket, some tar, some cheap mud bricks and get to work, with a smile on your face and a knowing nod to your noble, all-embracing cause. Heaven is just above the clouds. Utopia is yours – ours – for the taking.

If you think that this sounds a wee bit extremist, you would be correct. There are only so many ideologies to go round, and they will continue to go round, and in this regard the hardest of the Left is high-fiving the hardest of the Right where the horseshoe of politics curves towards the other. They always meet at that same vanishing point. All extremes converge in the end. They all have the same goal. Order always begets order. Ending one routine is never the end of routine, even ones that are forced or futile. Repeating this until we are blue in the face may be worth it in the end, even if you are personally sick of hearing it. I would hope not. For the increased division and dilution of us all is leading us dangerously back to Babel. That story is not a lament – it's a warning.

But if we did get there, and we are always getting there by one extreme or another, it will all end in the same way. There will be chaos, there will be blood, there will be brokenness.

And then there *will* be kin.

# Chapter 12: Slain



Have you been slain? I would think you probably have. Ask your kin, if you can find them; or if they are not lying dead on the blood-soaked battlefields of all our endeavours.

My direct and traceable family tree goes back several hundred years – at least that's where the spreadsheet stops. The summarised (and ever so slightly mythologised version) is that we were all peasant – and dare I say pleasant – farmers in north Yorkshire. There were quite a number of us scattered around the same area, and we did things in a certain way (the way kin does), including naming our first born. Out of nowhere, apparently, there arose a disagreement within our clan that the first born son should not be named in the same way as he had always been named (minority opinions exist in every group), and so the antagonist family in question broke the timeworn rule and – gasp – chose a different moniker for their wee laddy. The scandal spread like wildfire between the kin. Many were outraged, a few were indifferent. But the damage was done, and there followed an almighty split. Little George (that wasn't his name) had no idea of the fuss he had just caused.

Some of the families took themselves off to Portugal and married into royalty. While there, some also started a port and original sherry operation that still exists today, and long may it continue. As far as my own specific line goes, however, I remained a peasant farmer, but I am rather partial to a nice tot of my own sherry every now and again. My paternal grandparents always kept a bottle in the fridge. And at least a dozen or so in the pantry.

Like every kin throughout the ages, mine have been touched by tragedy, tumult and terror. Despite my gardening and farming roots, however, I do not have much of a green thumb, although I carry the traits of my forebears in many more ways than one. Who do I think I am? I am a lot of things, and the sum total of more parts than stars. I am comprised and compiled of adversity, anguish and affliction. I am slain. And so are you.

You, whose family was bruised. You, whose children were forced into adoption, sold into slavery, or taken into "care". Thrown into schools for the indigent and Indigenous, indolent and inept. Beaten, forsaken, broken, murdered, deemed as half-bred and considered worthless, expendable. Raped, tortured, and raped again. Bound with unbreakable ties to abandon all you called your own; your lands swept irrevocably from underneath your feet. Your traditions were purged and scourged, your ancient grounds desecrated, your light extinguished with the wrath of ages. Our kin forced themselves onto yours in ways and means unimaginable, but not untold, at least not now. Once terrified voices, cowed and controlled in the darkness, are speaking up and being heard. You who once were slain are rising with the dawn.

I wish the above summary – for want of any kind of appropriate word to encapsulate such horror in one brief paragraph – wasn't describing recent, or even current, events. But it is, and it always has. This is the story of our history and we are all slain within it. Perhaps God should have let us build that bloody tower after all.

"It's complicated" doesn't really come close, does it. But that's where we're at, and our best hopes of reconciling with each other in our giant sandbox seem to consist of throwing more sand in each other's faces – just a little less heartily than before, and with slightly less unkindness. That's maybe not the worst of outcomes, but generally where we are at present. Then more tragedy happens and the sandstorm arrives with raging fury yet again, and none of us can see each other, let alone the edges of the sandbox. As such, we need to feel our way around the exterior a little bit before we can try and make our way back to the centre.

Giving up ground, once we have it before us, is not something we have ever been good at, irrespective of how such ground was gained in the first place. For those of us who never had much ground to speak of – or whose distant ancestors had it ripped away from them at some point, too far away from us to ever know – we cling on to other things, perhaps more intangible, but nevertheless our own psychological "lands". And our lands have gates and boundaries and significance and burial places as sacred as any: of any class, culture, time or peoples. We are all bound and attached to our cultural, ancestral homes, hallways, hills and heaths in ways some of us are rarely in a position to consider, even if we were allowed to. Our sandbox is vast, but it's ours. Sharing it is simply not something we do naturally, except perhaps with our kin. The rest are just strangers. Aren't they?

To say that we all deserve to be treated the same, and should be treated the same, however, is nonsense, as unequivocally obnoxious as that may sound. The closest of kin don't even treat each other the same (and never have) so how it can even be considered a justifiable premise at a social or organisational level is completely erroneous. We are essentially unable to treat people in the same way, and we have no idea what we even mean when we drag out such spurious phrases anyway. If questioned, we'd probably talk about fairness or equality and hold up these words as having innate power and purity. Yet equality can only truly be quantified in how it appears, specifically when it relates to social inclusion or integration. And life just isn't fair. This is probably one of the reasons why we focused on equality of outcomes, as it's possibly a little easier to measure, even if it's all part of the same diaphanous ideology. Complicating matters further, we find plopped on top of our social and political arena the ambiguous and frightfully convoluted notions of multiculturalism, identity politics, diversity and inclusion, cultural integration, and all forms, modes and methods of each, as well as their inevitable offshoots, off-cuts and, occasionally, off the wall bits as well.

If we have a socialist (or even harder Left) inclination for example, to imply we can all exhibit the same classless, collective behaviour, but somehow retain our innate characteristics, in favour of a solidified, unified stateless society is a mind-boggling, self-defeating ideal, as simplistic as my analysis undoubtedly is. Multiculturalism and traditional forms of socialism don't seem like very compatible bedfellows on the face of it, which is probably one of the reasons why the hard

Left never really took much of a shine to multiculturalism in the first place. The hard Right didn't care for it either for reasons likely not too hard to imagine, so they had a quick confab with each other across that horseshoe, mutually decided to let the whole project fall by the wayside, and both went back to their subsequent planning rooms to regroup and rehash. The middle were also relieved by this outcome, even though we'd been quietly expressing our concerns for years.

The slightly more innocuous promotion of diversity and inclusion instead – by virtue of differences that apparently should be celebrated simply because they are different, not necessarily because they are worthy or worthwhile – still does not fit easily within our political or moral frameworks, even though variants of it have been shoehorned into our social and organisational institutions over a number of years, spawning plenty of debate, and disarray. In this regard, this is where diversity and inclusion issues occasionally segue into identity politics, creating splinter groups that have, over time, taken definitions of self-identification down to the level of the subatomic. Fueled by shared identities – often ones made up as if on the fly – groups can then homogenize (which in itself is a bit of an antithesis), feel even more marginalized, gain a louder voice, start a movement, and cry foul at their perceived inequalities and lack of integration. Yet identity politics is nothing more than a fiercer left wing, antagonistic derivative of multiculturalism, and deserves the same ignominious fate.

As an aside, proponents of socialism are probably still trying to work out how best to "include" diversity, inclusion and all those rising and falling identities in their methodology, so maybe that will continue to be in the making for them. All extremes have to adapt to the swiftness of change and the complexities of humanity, albeit often more from a vote-grabbing perspective than anything else. It's only when in power that those troublesome little citizens and their pesky little issues and identities can be dealt with properly.

Yet as much as we are strangers, we are all no strangers to what makes us the same. We're just not necessarily fond of what makes us different, and neither should we be "just because". While the idea of the cultural melting pot may seem to have been abandoned (by most), and the tone softened, we have only been able to rephrase it or redefine it. We couldn't ever get rid of it. We opted for the mosaic instead and determined that the richness of our difference would create a new and glorious picture, one that truly reflected the light of our social and organisational togetherness and enhanced understanding and appreciation of each other. But light refracts as well as reflects.

As our societies have grown more and more diverse, but less and less cohesive, the ongoing effect is the refraction and dissolution of national identity, and the threats – often carried out – to protect its destruction and disappearance. Diversity and inclusion policies would therefore appear to appeal to Leftist sensibilities more than the Right, but are not necessarily the exclusive weapon of either – only when it comes to gaining supporters. When taken to their fullest extremes, however, all diversity and inclusion have to offer society is no society to speak of – just the same melting pot of chaos all over again. For diversity and inclusion do not equal equality. A mosaic is as unequal as that melting pot, even if it looks a little bit better. There's about as much conflation in the whole mindset as I can cope with in one sentence, but it may be fair to say that if you iron out inequality, you iron out quite a lot of the reasons for what you were included for in the first place. We all become uniquely equal. At the very least, our now included diversity loses some of its essence, some of its edge. The mosaic is a crowded place after all. Even unicorns can't hide their disappointment when they enter a room full of other unicorns, which makes them want to be even more different unicorns than the others. Now there's a rabbit hole we've already gone down. We want to keep hold of our diversity as much as we yearn for inclusion and equality – but three really is a crowd.

Division, destruction, dilution, or separation of family, kin, group and clan is as much a trademark of one extreme as it is of another. Where one may be forced, through warfare, or other forms of violent takeover, the other is also forced – sometimes unwittingly, usually not – through rejection of social hierarchies, abolition of inequality and redistribution of "wealth". (Yes, this word is always rather ambiguous.) While one extreme may crush one kin, the other pretends to champion the cause of it, only to split it up when the time is right, iron it out so flat and thin it loses all meaning anyway, or ultimately control it with the same iron fist. Massacre, melting pot or mosaic – we don't ever seem to have much of a choice. In the end, total domination is the disposition of all extremes, and the result has never been good, on any scale.

Finding and keeping hold of the middle ground here is not a particularly straightforward process, which should hardly come as a surprise. We could therefore boil it down to a syrupy, outdated statement, phrased as a question: is there unity in diversity? To expand this even more, we can ask if there is unity in diversity and inclusion, as the latter word likes to hold hands with the former nowadays. It was as if diversity needed a more defined purpose, so we gave it one.

No. The answer is as short as that. The statement assumes facts not in evidence, which makes the question a loaded one. We're very good at being the morons when it comes to the oxymoron. We have never been united by our differences or by being included "just because". We know this somewhat instinctively, perhaps, which is why the concept was always deliberately a touch antithetical, but that didn't appear to stop us from pressing ahead with the same kind of beliefs anyway. Nowadays it's the bread and butter of our daily subsistence, and sometimes the only meal we're fed. Only this time it's not really about unity – that word is a bit gauche nowadays, even for some of the fluffiest and flakiest of us. It's more about behaving like we all get along – being welcoming, obliging, respectful and fair. Don't we just love our mosaic? This surely is the best the middle has to offer. But we can't be forced, or even expected, to play nicely in that sandbox. It may be nice but it isn't kind. And it therefore isn't natural. If neither of these things, it will fail catastrophically. Again.

For as much as talking about diversity, inclusion, culture, class, heritage, identity, race – any words that are relevant within the same realm of discussion – are indeed worthy of such discussion, they were never supposed to occupy the level of the intellectual in quite the manner they do. For they do not inhabit our minds at a deliberately cerebral level when we are the ones presenting our issues and concerns, in whatever heartfelt manner we choose to do so. To us, they are instinctual, intrinsic and inherent. And therefore extremely sensitive, sensual and special, if largely intangible. We cannot detach ourselves emotionally from them. Any resulting academic debate is as impersonal, high-fallutin and convoluting – and thereby irrelevant – to us as anyone else. As such, any skin-deep, theoretical promotion of diversity and inclusion, and all that is invested and divested therein, can only reek of ulterior motivation. One of the sole reasons we seek to understand something is so that we can command it. Or them. For we made these issues academic and intellectual so that we could control and manipulate them, fabricate and manufacture them, and thereby turn them into tools of social and organisational engineering.

It's one of our most unkind ways of behaving, in the nicest ways possible.


Which brings us back in a somewhat roundabout fashion to Jeremiah and a quick gear change. *Oh, that my head were a spring of water and my eyes a fountain of tears! I would weep day and night for the slain of my people.*

If history has taught us anything at all, it's that we all mourn and weep for our people, our kin. When tragedy or terror befalls us, we wail and lament. And we yearn for the day when we will rise again and claim our rightful place, our rightful heritage, our rightful inheritance and our rightful lands. If we are white, we tend to struggle with the land part because we were probably the ones who took it from the people who are weeping in the first place – from many of them in their living memory. It was theirs, now it's ours, and we're stuck. If we're black, we rise up against the tyranny of slavery and racial inequality, and demand concessions for both of these evils, mainly from those who are white. There's rage, movements, protests, violence, social media meltdown. Lots of sand in our eyes at this point. Lots and lots of sand. Our usual gritty, grainy gridlock.

I write the above in a somewhat detached-sounding and simplistic manner for one reason, and one reason alone: it is that simple. The issues aren't, by any stretch of the imagination, but the responses are. They are always the same, and will simply continue to be the same. They will repeat themselves throughout history in every continent, country and county, and in every class, culture and civilization, because they already have. Past behaviour predicts future behaviour. To comment on this is easy. What follows isn't.

Without protests, without movements, without the fires of outrage burning, without banners, marches, blockades, finger-pointing, fuss-fanning, blame-assigning, shame-sharing, name-calling, self-isolation, self-flagellation, self-importance and self-satisfaction; without every tactic we have ever employed – or could ever employ – to make our grief and grievances known, we are all still slain. The chaos is inevitable and irreversible. What we have lost is irretrievable. And we prefer to measure our lives with what we did have and what we don't have, rather than what we do. As such, we can barely place any value on ourselves, let alone anyone else. That's the true betrayal of inclusion, integration, and all policies alike – they gradually steal away from us everything we had left, to the point we can only weep and wail for our kin. If we no longer know who we are, we will long for who we were.

We have all been slain. That's our starting point. Sadly, it appears to be our vanishing point as well. But this was chapter 12 for a reason.

# Chapter 13: Right

*When the storm has swept by, the wicked are gone, but the righteous stand firm forever.*

*Proverbs 10:25*

Being right is helpful, particularly during Monday night trivia at our local watering hole. One of the prizes was once a fondue set. We didn't win it. We only got 8 out of 18 in that particular round. But I don't think righteousness cares too much about those kinds of questions. It's not there to help us win cheap, inferior treasures. It's got more on its mind than trivia. Shame that we don't sometimes. I like fondue.

In the first sentence of chapter 1 there is a small slice of my vitae. It seemed a reasonable enough way to start things off. Regardless of the jobs I've had since my few years spent bumbling around at the front of a classroom, however, one thing remains evident – we love being right. It is both the flagstones of our path and the flagpoles of our palace, and without doubt the flagship of our fleet. Whichever way it is phrased, we derive great satisfaction waving our rightness around like a flag – a giant flag bearing a colossal unicorn. It gives us confidence and cheer. And it makes us behave in all sorts of weird and wonderful ways. Mostly weird, if we're honest. If not, downright obnoxious.

In a latter role I once fielded a phone call from a very disgruntled client. She lambasted me furiously for all the things that I should have done, could have done, and would now do for her without question. She didn't just hit the roof, she whacked it repeatedly with a very large and heavy broom handle. She told me in multiple ways that I wasn't doing my job, concluded she could do it better than me, and then said I would be hearing from her lawyer. She wasn't wrong.

A few minutes later her lawyer called. She was like her client but with more spikes. She – and I don't say this lightly – yelled at me viciously for my neglect of her client, and tried to cross-examine me on all the things I had done, hadn't done and should, in her eyes, be doing right now. She didn't just hit the roof, she shot like a rocket from the chimney into the stratosphere. Having been cross-examined many times before, I was fortunately able to maintain my nice, polite demeanour. But I do think I quietly hung up before she landed.

After this, I called a male client – separated husband of the female client – and he hit the roof too. She was a liar! How could I even entertain such fiction, slander and distortion of facts. And he hung up in disgust. Then his lawyer called me, and he hit the roof as well. At this point, I was also levitating perilously towards the ceiling fan. I'm clearly out of metaphors here, as well as slightly mythologising facts again to keep things interesting. There wasn't really a ceiling fan. In any case, as the story goes, all of us five dear souls were now mutually and animatedly elevated. Common ground, let alone the actual ground, did not appear to be anywhere in sight. And the "she" and "he" aspects of this tale are without myth by the way, if you feel that there may be some gender bias going on. Both were awful, if that helps.

You don't have to have held an employment position where you regularly have one person screaming in one ear to do one thing, and another person screeching in your other ear to do another, to know how this all feels. You can put that job on your vitae, but it's a room full of unicorns nevertheless. This is a widespread human condition. We just love that instant floor to ceiling experience. We really want to be right.

"Right" is a complicated word. We treat it as if it wasn't, but it has nuances infused into our collective anthology and anthropology that we could never quantify. It would be well deserving of its own book – or set of books – but for our purposes we have a relatively pithy chapter titled in its honour. And we tend to get really pithy when we aren't right – with ourselves, as much as with everyone else.

One of the many ancient birthplaces of the term *right* is, perhaps a touch unsurprisingly, *righteousness*. For all the synonyms, phrases, explanations and demonstrations of *right* exhibited in every class, culture and civilization throughout the millennia allude to a moral construct or code – nothing whatsoever to do with the presentation of random pieces of information in order to proudly walk away with a fondue set. The more globalized we have become, those ancient moral constructs and codes have often been forgotten or forsaken, and we've had to largely reinvent what we consider *right* to be in our melting pot or mosaic. For the most part, our new sense of right is supposed to apply to everyone. It's our contemporary and collective moral code.

Yet, despite this, we're certainly not always inclined towards the righteous – more like the self-righteous – when we thrust our visions and versions of correctness on others, but that is to be expected. We never obtained perfection under any former construct. For the most part we can figure that out, particularly when we afford ourselves the opportunity to sit down, shut up, sober up, and sort out the jumbled mess of our own thoughts. Doing that in this noisy, cluttered, confusing world of ours isn't exactly a pleasure, so this is where we often rely on the rightness of others to add fuel to our little fires, hence our tendency to cut selected snippets of other people's vitae and paste them onto our own arguments. That method, as previously encountered, isn't something we do very well either. As such, being right should probably entail more of the sit, sober and *shh* than it typically does. Now there's three things that work well together if we would let them, and I am most certainly preaching to myself here too.

Talking of preaching and being right – yes, you've got it. Cigars. Couldn't leave it alone, could I. But this is my book and I have not written it for you. (I mean that kindly – a dedication is a dedication after all.) You'll get over it in the fullness of time. In the meantime, imagine you are a policy-maker, or a law-maker, or even that Elder from Babel before it all went pear-shaped. Whoever you are, you are now the fulcrum upon which a wide-ranging decision tips one way or the other.

On the one hand – or rather in the one ear – you have people screaming that smoking is dangerous, unhealthy, disgusting and damaging. Second-hand smoke is egregiously unfair to those who inhale it, and the cost of dealing with smoking-related health conditions is a tremendous financial burden on the whole nation. It must therefore all come to an end. This is absolutely right.

In the other ear, the arguments vary in coherence, but they are still being screeched. Smoking is a personal choice. Sugar is worse for you (conflation, yes, but possibly also true). Second-hand smoke is not proven to be as bad as it is claimed to be. You can smoke away from people anyway and therefore it doesn't affect them whatsoever. Smoking is legal, an ancient practice, and beneficial in other ways. Besides, don't those tobacco tax dollars more than account for the health stuff anyway? You can add more fuel (and plenty more conflation) to these fires – you've heard these points before. And all of this is absolutely right. So make your decision: ban smoking outright, or not. And you have to make that decision *now*. Do it.

You may have already done this before the arguments reached your eyeballs or your ears. You probably personalised it a bit. No, you definitely personalised it a lot. I certainly did, which is why I brought it up again in the first place. As we have previously glossed over, smoking is still a thing. But as you now have to make a choice between "yes" or "no" for a whole country, you are in very scary territory. This is on you. The nation is waiting. You are hugely exposed. Good luck. At this point, I think I'd rather be Matt.

We are continually imploring our leaders to be right, or rather to do the right that we want them to do. *Do the right thing.* And while there are many sides to an argument, decision-making often boils down to a choice between two options, i.e. two sides: yes or no. If it doesn't – if there is any kind of neutral middle ground – it's the lack of yes and no that is still picking a side. As a decision-maker you simply can't win for the most part, but there is always a side that feels that they have. And the winning part is what makes people believe they were right in the first place – it validates their existing beliefs and opinions. We like to throw grit on the road behind us as proof of why we didn't slip over.

But being right does not equal doing right, and vice versa. While one unicorn's meat may be another unicorn's poison, if there was no meat to begin with we'd all be vegetarian and the idiom would perhaps involve carrots. And there is a difference between unicorn's meat and unicorn meat. The latter just isn't right and would make children cry. The point being, there isn't one anywhere in this paragraph so far. It's a collection of nonsense, and I'm right to say that. For more often than not, our modern interpretation of being right is an exercise in pointing out the obvious without ever really making any kind of point, and being flippant, silly and rude all at the same time. That's pretty much what comedy consists of. And the details that make up our points are usually trivia anyway. All told, we're not really being right, per se, just observational and opinionated – that's the sum total of how right we are, most of the time. That's us. It's our comedy of error.

Highlighting facts – or what we see as factual – is one of our favourite forms of being right. How can you argue with the facts? With trillions of facts of all shapes and sizes now at our fingertips we can be right whenever we want – how lucky we are. Even though using a mobile phone during Monday night trivia is a crime worthy of being sent to the Tower (yes, this would be right), for the most part we are allowed to call upon those facts whenever we want. We literally don't have to use our hands. Or, as it turns out, our minds as well.

It is a very self-deflating existence to have every fact we could ever need right there when we need them. Who wants to spend a lifetime walking in front of an eternal row of dusty old-fashioned textbooks on a shelf. It's taken a lot of the fun out of being right, and a lot of the fight with it. It narrowed down the debate to an electronic echo chamber filled with inflatable weaponry. So we created new forms of fighting instead. Order is always replaced with order. And it is because we got very bored with this existence we invented a whole load of new facts to make things a little bit more festive and feisty. Our new facts spawned their own facts and multiplied like cells – the online world made this happen extremely quickly. In doing so, we rewrote our own history by virtue of diluting everything that has ever happened to the point that it lost its taste. And we sure like to be tasteless.

We can no longer examine our heritage, our story, our myths, our ancient fables, without that all-pervasive infusion of our new facts. We spoiled them. We defiled them. We flooded them with so many new parts, plots, characters and, of course, commentary on behaviours, that they've lost their magic. And we're not allowed to hark back to any kind of halcyon days, or misty far off lands, or past glories, as these are now suffused, if not wholly whitewashed, with our newly begotten facts. It's as if our collective notions of righteousness have become a giant game of trivia, with the prizes on offer being just as naff as they ever were. And all because we just wanted to be right. It was self-loathing that spawned our new righteousness, and that is why it can only be loathed.

We're a bunch of loathsome, fact-flinging fools. We can even spend whole wads of time feverishly and fiercely debating facts that we just made up on the spot – like inventing something, only to then blame it for existing. For there is an element within us that so despises our own existence we can see the results and ramifications of this wherever we look, if we had our eyes open. To offset this enormous shame, we try so hard to be right.

Whether or not it makes us feel any better appears largely moot. For the most part we don't even know we're doing it. We've smacked our heads on the roof so many times we are dazed and desensitized beyond all manner of reason. Being right hurts. So does being righteous. But we opted solely for the former.

Any mob or movement believes that they are right – indeed even righteous. When the cause appears virtuous, this justifies all means in their eyes. Yet for every hundred people out there screaming, shaming, blaming and trying their hardest to unhinge every gate post, there are hundreds of thousands sitting at home observing the news and shaking their heads in dismay. (I have no idea of the actual statistics – it matters not.) We know that the mob is the minority – online or off – but they have still forced us to bow the knee. We have capitulated for years in so many contexts that we cave in time after time, even when faced with nothing more than anarchy. We gave ourselves little option to do anything else as our policies and procedures backed up our concessions and ultimate surrender anyway. We had tried so hard to be right, we weren't. Not even close. Now we have no idea what to do. This is as dangerous as it is debilitating, as well as incredibly destabilizing.

Something is clearly amiss. Something just isn't right.

# Chapter 14: Good

*Everyone has turned away, all have become corrupt; there is no one who does good, not even one.*

*Psalm 53:3*

There is a fundamental difference between being good and doing good. We are that difference. Our individual souls are the fulcrum upon which the everlasting scale rests, and it is always on us. Soul sludge doesn't help the scale move in the righteous direction, if we decided to investigate our intentions with any level of searing, searching honesty.

Being right = doing good? Doing good = being right? We never seem able to balance the equation. In light of the previous chapter, we appear to have largely run out of options. We always find ourselves back at square one. And that's where we hit the bottle of all our failed plans, foiled hopes and faked promises. At this stage, any suitably robust word starting with "f" is more than fitting. We really fluff things up. I do. We do. You do. They do. We are patently, pathetically and primordially incapable of doing good. Yet we do some really good stuff. How on earth do we juggle that ugliest, most detestable of paradoxes while sober?

Some exceptionally narcissistic, evil, predatory, abusive, violent and malevolent characters have "done" a lot of good throughout our history. Some molested and raped generations of children for decades, while simultaneously pouring generous funds into charities, setting up hospitals, worthy institutions and benevolent societies. Did they do good? I can see why some statues could and should be toppled. We all can, but we are still only screaming hatred at ourselves. We can cast them into the abyss, but we can never recast our past. There are famed and fabled names who helped people, treated people, saved people, and made the world a better place. They "did good". They brought about positive change. They were heroes and pioneers, yet exhibited the worst of all our sordid and salacious tendencies, often leaving behind concealed and camouflaged trails of the worst and most hideous of human depravities. And when these things come to light, if they were not apparent at the time, the blunt force trauma to our communal conscious leaves us crushed, demoralised and in deepest chasms of despair.

It's a sword through the heart of all of us – yet one which we help to sharpen by our own nature, and it hurts beyond all measure of time and essence. It just isn't good. It is pain of eternal consequence. It excoriates the fragile membrane of our conscience and leaves us standing exposed in the darkness of all our most terrifying, infernal nightmares.

We are all slain.


No, this is not where I suddenly announce an answer and pop a cork dramatically from the celestial Champagne bottle of hope and glory. I do not carry deliverance and salvation around in my satchel. Come to think of it, I haven't even got a satchel. It's a duffle bag in my walk-in closet. My wife bought it for me for

Christmas one year. I use it for clothing, washroom sundries and various other personal detritus while away from home. So we could perhaps use this as a starting point. Not my duffle bag, as such, more like our own universal baggage. We all carry around the same stuff.

If you've ever uttered, or heard uttered, a phrase along the lines of: *I'm sorry ... I've got a lot going on*, this would be perhaps one of the most widely-used but most understated personal realisms of our times. We really do have a lot going on. When hemmed in on all sides by our clutter, confusion, consternation and chaos, our mental processes suffer, if not break down, and our ability to distribute vital emotional resources to each area of concern in our minds is severely impeded, if not impossible. As such, often the best we can offer is a one-size-fits-all apology, with a one-fact-fits-all reasoning – we have a *lot* going on.

The more we unpack and unpick what we have going on, the more we realise we don't even know specifically what was bothering or upsetting us, even if we cherry-picked a reason to justify why we felt bad, or more likely acted badly, on any given occasion. *My mother is sick, my father is in hospital, my pet died, my child is being bullied, financial problems, health concerns, separation and divorce, childhood trauma.* The rest of this chapter, let alone this paragraph, could be a long list of all our personal issues, angst and anguish, and we typically cannot extract any one reason from a list that is often as comprehensive as this for any of us at any time as cause for why we reacted and screamed in the first place. It could be anything. The more we have going on, the less we know what is doing the most damage. It all hurts. Yet as much as we try and compartmentalise things, and tuck our most painful of past or present issues into our brain boxes, we have no control over the lids. They flip open whenever they want, and spill their agonizing contents into the delicately assembled order of our soulful existence time and again. Everything overlaps and envelops us eventually.

And it is this realisation – implicit or not – that we also tend to try and cut this off at the pass: anything to circumvent (or even perhaps deny) the lid-flipping that is going on inside our minds. So we like to make it other people's fault if it happens, or advise them that it will be – if they don't follow our strictest and most specific of instructions to begin with. It's not difficult, and we do it rather a lot.

We can let people know our triggers and tipping points. We can lay them all out before us like a school science project: circuit boards of our conscious, sensitive switches (actually, let's make that hypersensitive), fussy fuse boxes and rousing resistors. All the things that we know will set us off. While we have always been very good at poking the bear in each other, the modern version of this has inverted the process. We don't have to get to know anyone any more. We can present our bears for the non-poking to anyone, even strangers. For whole swathes of people nowadays – colleagues, acquaintances, friends (online or off), or even vast sections of society – we can so bravely and conveniently slap our personal circuitry down in front of them and dare them not to press our buttons. Here's my triggers – don't even think about it. I can see you thinking about it. You thought about it. Now you're in the wrong and I'm upset. You flipped my lid. We will do whatever it takes to offset and offload our deepest, darkest fears and frustrations. Our brave face is anything but.

Yet nestled between the disquiet and the discomfort of our own souls are little patches of harmony that we have always carried with us. They are the residue of peoples and places, times and spaces. They are inherent in all of us, if we care to seek them out. Often we try, but we have to make an extra special effort, and employ increasingly pronounced – but nonetheless mindful – tactics such as ensuring our pillowcases are treated with a veneration and devotion hitherto unknown in the history of laundry, or by sticking tiny needles between our toes. (I have a peculiar fear of, and fascination with, acupuncture.) It is difficult to sometimes put our finger on these intrinsic harmonies, which is why we come up with specific strategies to find them, and have done so for countless generations, throughout every culture. It's also why I prefer doing the washing over being a human porcupine. It's a gate thing.

A number of years ago my wife and I were driving through the Okanagan in the interior of British Columbia, Canada. It is beautiful there. I recall having a somewhat strange reaction to the hills and mountains that I couldn't quite place. I felt I'd been there before, even though on that particular trip, I hadn't. Without sounding too ethereal or like I've been smoking something other than, you know what, the place spoke to me. It still does, even in a Toyota Yaris.

Some years later, we were driving in Scotland. It wasn't in a Yaris. But as majestic hills loomed before us out of the inevitable mist, I felt that same tangible sense of knowing, of resonant belonging, but even more potent. I felt I'd been there before too, although I don't believe I'd ever been to that particular area, but my first thought was: *wow, this place reminds me of the Okanagan.* And then, the more I thought about it, the more I came to realise that it wasn't the hills of Scotland that brought to bear latent memories of Canada, but vice versa. Here, in the northern part of that sceptered isle were my own intractable roots. The source of my surname. The ancient birthplace of my very soul. Here was *my* land. My gates, walls, fences and fields. Here were my kin: memories of peoples and places, times and spaces. The unity and harmony between us all, and between all things. A sense of being. A sense of who we really are. A sense of home.

But I can never go back. Yes, I can visit. When my working days are done (that is, my pensionable hours sorting out other people's problems), I could even go and live there. Obviously I'd take my wife, or she'd be rather disappointed. After all, on that same trip to Scotland, we visited the graves of her own ancestors, her age-old kin, in a tiny walled cemetery outside of Inverness. We found ourselves together in more ways than one. And once retired, together, we could put down new roots in our ancestral homeland, even if by then we were worn and grey and ready to ring the final bell. We're already definitely quite worn, and the grey started to happen a while ago. And given the myriad uncertainties of life, our chances of such blissful re-emergence into our essence blow away like ash in the wind every day that passes. We can never really go back. No one can.

We steal a lot from each other. Not my wife and I – this is a new paragraph and the context has shifted. We also move on and leave behind what we had, even if we took it from someone and somewhere else, in some long-forgotten age. Our universal baggage is an unholy mess of timeworn cloth, woven together in fractal patterns, interspersed with confused and haphazard stitching where cultures and civilizations collide, intertwine, and explode violently outwards across the whole, leaving runs and trails and threads to nowhere, scorch marks, and areas too burned or threadbare to discern. We are the sands in ours and each other's hourglass, and the hands on the handles that reset the balance.

In all we have and all we are, we cannot do the good we want to do. It's not that we are incapable of it, but we don't know what "it" is. We have an inherent notion, personal and private though those notions may be, or vomited onto the pages of history by those who were not so private, but we often work out what was good for us in hindsight, rather than decide at the time that our actions are pure and perfect. We find, more often than not, that the pure and the perfect at the time turns out to be nothing more than ulterior motive, yearning for power, control, gluttony, greed and then final, heartbreaking despair. Yet we can find the good, if we look for it. We can see that silver lining in the thunderous clouds of all our efforts – fake, flawed and foul. And that appears to be the sum total of it: doing the best we can in the midst of the chaos; making do with the tips and the tools to hand. Seeking order, trying to be reasonable rather than right. We do not, for the most part, seriously believe we are doing good, not if we ever sit sober and silent and face the discordant music of all our intentions, and all our fallacy of form and function.

There has only ever been one equation that serves as the balance between all we have, all we were, and all we ever can be. It is not subject to class, race, culture, tribe, tongue or unicorn. It is the starting point and the vanishing point, the crux of it all. It is the balance between all things, on those everlasting scales.

Being good = doing good. It is the absolute dividing line between Order and Chaos; the infinite separation of soul and spirit. It is truth, the very word of it, and the light unto our bleakest of paths.

# Chapter 15: Light

*God saw that the light was good, and he separated the light from the darkness.*

*Genesis 1:4*

There are two creation stories in the book of Genesis. The first is usually prefaced with two rather unambiguous words: *The Beginning.* The second story, as much as it intertwines with the first, is the one with the unclothed couple in the Garden of Eden – the tale of Adam, his rib, Eve, an insidious serpent, a couple of important trees, a fruit, some obvious (and obviously bad) decision-making, some shame, blame, falling from grace, and there we all are staring at our mobile phones. Clearly rather a lot has happened between these mighty epochs in our social and emotional histories.

As much as my gates – and those of others – might creak in protest, or slam shut in our faces with a rebuking *thunk*, these stories are not the same account of the same thing, nor were they ever intended as such. Neither were they supposed to engender that inevitable and age-old debate over whether or not they are fact or fiction. They are mythological narratives, pure and simple. Myths are a mechanism for delivery, yet we often focus way too much on how the delivery occurred, rather than what arrived. It's like bickering incessantly with each other over which courier delivered a parcel – without ever opening the parcel. These stories are, however, rather wonderful if we choose to interrogate them with even the most basic of questions, while simultaneously examining the package before us. We already briefly encountered the naked folks in an earlier chapter, so let us look closely and crisply at the opening notes of the beginning – the first of our days, the very first of songs.

Myth, fable, legend – however you want to spin it around or spit it out, the reason "God" separated the light from the darkness is relevant to the fabric our being, if not the framework of this chapter. Yet it's not a question that is usually asked. So why would God do such a thing? Why did he insert light into the darkness, rather than banish all darkness forever? Again, the question of his existence is utterly irrelevant to the existence of the question. If we cannot ask, we cannot answer. If we don't ask, we don't know. Myths were designed to be chewed over, not chucked away. Who knows, maybe in a few more millennia, if we're still here in one striated form or another, there will be some kind of unicorn legend giving us a sense of who we are and where we came from. Perhaps it doesn't even matter. We'd probably remain quite unsure of where we were going, and still fretting about how we were to get to that unseen, unknowable location in the first place. We've never dealt with uncertainty very well. We're kind of pathetic really. Or just paranoid.

Genesis 1:4 is the first time the word *good* is mentioned in the Book. It is immediately preceded by the word *light*, and just before light, *darkness*. I am comforted by the expediency of this story and the way in which light (and therefore goodness) arrived with such swift and eternal conviction. Only four verses in and at least we can see what we're doing, even if we haven't got a clue what it is we are supposed to be doing.  Light is good, but darkness remained with us. It wasn't destroyed – just maybe delayed. Thank goodness it was never all there was. If the Bible was only these four verses, it might not be too bad for us, but things could never be that unstructured. Not a bad start though.

Perhaps our inescapable role is to separate the light from the darkness too.  If we are made in the image of a creator, or through what evidently came into being (somehow, some when), we are nevertheless bound by immutable laws etched so deeply into the particles of existence, we cannot evade or escape them, even if we decide that our purpose is pointless and we are destined for the chaos and oblivion that preceded all things anyway. The earliest of thinkers and "writers" (in every context of this word; in every scratch, scar, carving, glyph and inscription) apparently thought along the same lines. They hadn't got a clue either, but they were searching. For the most part they preferred illumination over elimination. They liked light.

There are no answers here – just pointers.  Markers along the way. Blazes on the trails. For we are all drawn inexorably towards the light, and some of us even like to pretend we've been exposed to it by spraying ourselves in varying shades of tan, in order to depose the pallid, peaky presence of living without the sun. And when the sun emerges, we rush out into its warm, lovely rays, ever desperate to be in that ancient, storied place of goodness.  As far as I am aware, it wasn't the darkness that was ever supposed to be good.  I would take issue with any myth that claimed otherwise. If you would too, I think we've found a relatively decent starting point, which is probably why this particular creation story – as with so many others like it – started off in the way that it did. Light is good; darkness sucks. Those five words could start their own religions.

As a child I was terrified of the dark. Even now, I have an ambivalent relationship with the night time. My beloved wife is the same with her restless legs and restless brain. We are two peas in a pod, even if we tag team throughout the wee hours in being awake or asleep. Talking of wee hours, I am typically conscious at 2am, still at work in my mind, and then a brief trip to the washroom and a glass of water generally helps reset that legendary thing known as "a good night's sleep", and I drift off a short while later, only to have dreams as exhausting as being awake. Darkness sucks. God didn't create it, after all. No one did.

We don't know why we sleep, but we know we probably have to. Perhaps there is some intrinsic knowledge – if that's the right choice of word – that when the darkness falls, we might as well take a break until the sun pokes its glorious face above the horizon. Maybe the night was always supposed to be the time when we shut down, shut up, and shut off the lights, even though our dreams often make us more wakeful and fretful than we are during the day. Staring at a little bright screen for hours while lying there possibly doesn't help matters either. In the grand scheme of things, all scheming aside, the night is not there to bring us pain and suffering. Yet how it has, and how it does. Perhaps even "God" couldn't do anything about that.

In that old workplace of mine – the same office that had the computer mouse exposition posted to a cork board for a quarter of a century – a former colleague, a lawyer, said some terrible words. They weren't her words – she was quoting what had happened in court, but they have shattered me hence. She was assisting an Indigenous client who had attended years before, not by choice, a residential school for him and his despised, displaced kin. Not that schools themselves tend to be optional, but there are those certain institutions that have enslaved, deprived and bankrupted generations of the most precious souls from anything even remotely resembling an education. Sometimes the word systemic doesn't even come close to describing the horror. Her client, in trying his best to explain the immeasurable pain of his experiences, said: *they came for my friends in the night.* And she said to me, with a look that fells trees: *I think he was talking about himself.* When trauma so grievous and so malevolent is brought into the light, to speak about it in the third person was probably the best he could have done. Some things cannot be unheard, and some things cannot be undone. And we have done evil in the darkness, and we will continue to do so. Evil loves the night.

It has only been a couple of centuries since electric light became a thing in our lives, and about half that time since the widespread use of such light in our homesteads and habitats. Prior to this, light was messy, smelly and often dangerous in its human application and delivery. After all, it was fire. In many respects, it still is.

Our relationship with the light, and with the trillions of fires that illuminated us for countless generations across all divides before we plugged ourselves in to the mainframe, is not something we can readily flush from our system, even if we wanted to. When we go camping, we don't all throw our mobile phones into a pit with the brightness set to max and enjoy their radiating warmth and glow, as the dusk falls and the air grows cooler. We like the real thing – the crackling of wood, the red-hot, white-hot embers; that unmistakable, ancient scent of burning, and the penetrating heat that radiates outwards towards our outstretched palms, our faces ever turned to the light. A hot dog on a stick and a refreshing adult beverage also work wonders too. We can't help ourselves – we are drawn to fire, to light; we are bound to it, saved by it. Call it evolutionary, a survival instinct, a deep-seated companionship beyond our words, but we know it, and feel it, and long for it. We do not wish to dwell in the darkness. For many of us, the morning simply can't arrive quickly enough. We need the dawn. We need that sun to rise once more, and banish into the abyss those fears and frights of all our darkest nights. No light bulb could ever come close. And then when dusk falls, it happens all over again. Light and dark were separated from each other for a reason.

And that reason is us. After all, if you are "God", it's always day somewhere and always night somewhere else. He's not the one getting up at 2am for a glass of water and some bladder relief. We can't control the passage of time, the waxing and waning of the moon, the tides, but we can exert some measure of righteous stewardship over our existence and over the world around us in order to hold back the darkness. We cannot destroy it, or preclude it, or change its nature, but we can repel it, reject it, and repudiate it with all of our being. We can choose to be a light in the gloomiest, most abysmal of places, but we cannot stop the chaos from being what it is. However we phrase it, or however we play with the words, the concepts or the realities, we can't do what God himself didn't do. Even the earliest of myth-writers understood this, or they'd have painted a better picture. *And God completely destroyed the darkness and we all lived happily ever after, but be sure to bring sunglasses to the party.*

*The End.*

You could probably start a whole religion or two with those few words as well, perhaps with the exception of the glory goggles, but as much as may be promised a happy and satisfying ending, no one can ever say they know for sure what lies beyond the veil, other than it may very well involve a whole lot of light. As far as endings go, however, this doesn't sound too awful. Maybe there really is a light at the end of the tunnel.

And it is unto this end – where all of our tunnels converge – that we will take a final trip back to the classroom. Not the one where we are still children, but the one where we never really left even when we grew up, and can never leave. We can put away childish things, but we cannot stop the child in all of us from crying out in the darkness, or throwing ourselves on the ground during the day in tantrums of disgust and despair when things don't go our way. Growing up has always been one of our most ironic, if not iconic, of claims.

We are all sitting at a table with each other during lessons, or sitting in a sandbox during break. And neither work time nor play time make any significant difference to who we are or how we behave. We are always rushing back into our classroom at the sound of the bell: jostling, pinching, blaming and shaming – telling tales, breathless, red-faced, wound up, seeking validation, assurance, and desperate for the rules to be enforced. None of us grow up from that stuff, but we do tend think to think we're too old for sitting cross-legged the carpet.

We cannot recuse ourselves from our own nature, from the chaos, from the darkness that swirls around us, and within us. Yet our nature also demands, deserves and desires order. We seek the balance; we seek the light. For it is in the light, and the light alone, that we must present the best, and the worst, of all of us: our nature, our choices, our plans and our perils. Everything in the end will be exposed. Everything, as it were, will come to light. How we choose to arrive at this final terminal of our souls is up to us. It always has been, and always will be. And it will not be pretty for any of us. For that's the thing about light – it didn't arrive to replace the darkness, or to repair it.

It came to reveal it and renounce it. And then, at the very end of all things, to remove it.

*Forever.*

# Chapter 16: Green, Blue, Yellow, Red (Part II)

*All the tables are covered with vomit and there is not a spot without filth.*

*Isaiah 28:8*

That's a shame. And there was me thinking that my Yellow table was largely free of desecration. Being such a good, hard-working and mindful bunch of children, surely my group at least was going to make it out unscathed. We could always blame the mess on the Green Group, couldn't we?

After all, they are the noisy, expensive and conspicuous ones. You can see them everywhere you go, even those lurking in the shadows. They never learned to hide particularly well. There they are and there they go – pushing their rattling carts and trolleys down the streets, stumbling and cursing, muttering and mumbling. They're the ones wigging out in full sight of the shoppers, or half collapsed in shop doorways drunk and incapable, urine soaked and stinky. Their brains, their minds rewired through devastating substance misuse – where choice is no longer any part of the process. They lost that battle years ago.

They collect their welfare cheques, ranting at the staff behind the screens, scratching open sores and tottering away into chaos: self-neglect, self-abuse, self-harm and absolute self-abandon. There's no bank accounts in their world – cheques are cashed and spent within hours, and then they subsist on the outermost fringes of reality until the next hand out, bail out or blow out. Their lives are a blur and a bondage; a shade, a slavery, a curse. They are on the far side of the classroom, the outskirts of all hope, and all of humanity along with it. They are lost.

But not all Greens ended up here. At least some made it to jail for a time, where they cleaned up their act, but soon got released and went straight back to their old ways. They're not living on the streets, but they scour them for victims and opportunities, often under cover of darkness, in order to feed whatever habit they are driven by. They are the petty thieves, the robbers, the burglars by night. By day the same, if they can, but they do not rise until the afternoon. The morning sun is not their cue – it blinds them and befuddles them. They dwell in the darkness. They are the users and abusers, the career cons, cads, crooks and criminals. They take what they can, when they can, how they can. And they give nothing back but pain.

It is easy for any of us to congratulate ourselves that we aren't in the Green Group. Some of us even spend our whole careers picking up the pieces behind them. While blame, judgement and cynicism is unavoidable, we know that the reasons for their faults and failings are not wholly down to us, despite all our efforts of help and intervention. They were born into chaos, as were we all, but for them the chaos was worse, more intense, more fetid, more foul, with no order around them to provide safe shelter. They were not shielded from the start, even while in the womb, and the poor choices of others along with the frameworks they were not permitted to construct at an early age fostered their own inability to choose wisely, fuelled by the bane of addiction, mental health breakdown, brain injury, cognitive deficits and lack of insight. There are no stereotypes here – just broken people, bound by fate to the darkness of all our wrongs and all our failed plans. They will always be there on the farthest of edges, caught up and entangled helplessly in the weeds.

But this chapter is not about the Greens. After all, they're not the ones likely to be reading this book, at least not the very worst of them. Whether you like it or not, you are the mainstream. If you've got this far, you made it there yourself, and you're still floating along. So have you picked your table already? Do you know where you sit? And do you even want to be in the mainstream? That's the kicker, and the question of questions for every Blue, Yellow and Red. So let's begin.

You are Blue, and you chose to follow a rocky road when you were younger. You possibly dabbled here and there as a young teenager with alcohol, truancy, trespass, a few drugs, and you ran from the law on more than one occasion – but not for anything heinous. You were into high jinks more than major crime. You didn't really want to upset people, but you couldn't help poking the bear and seeing what chaos had to offer. Your dyslexia or distractions didn't help your grades and you loved being outside, and being away from the classroom, yet you always fostered a strong sense of identity and some subjects really floated your boat. You weren't as thick as you acted. You have a good heart – displayed often on your sleeve – despite being a right little oik from time to time. You have plenty of gates, even if you have carelessly left some open, or spent your time swinging around on them and having a laugh with your friends. Your parents despaired, but you made it through. You somehow didn't end up on the wrong side of the bars, and now there you are putting the really bad ones behind them, or doing your best to save them. You also enjoy working with your hands in a skilled trade and being your own person. You are a police officer, a custody officer, a corrections officer, a health care worker, a plumber, electrician, carpenter, mechanic, ship builder. You joined the Forces. You still love a good drink and your spelling remains atrocious, but you are the life and the soul of the party and the salt of the earth. You don't care much about policies and procedures – at least not the stupid and unrealistic ones dreamed up by The Management in their vaulted ivory towers. They don't understand grunt work. You're out there every day, doing the stuff that gets the most attention on social media when something goes wrong and putting things right when the poop hits the fan. You just want to get things done. You probably know Matt, and what happened to him has really hacked you off.

You are Yellow. You are a sensitive soul. You cared about what the teacher thought and hated getting into trouble. Behaving like a Blue might have given you a thrill here and there, but you never pushed the envelope as far as they could. You liked writing, reading and social studies. Maths was not always your strongest subject, but you could get on with it and it often surprised you when you understood it. History was great, Geography was interesting, Sciences were fun. You were an all-rounder, and you had your favourites, but your biggest fears were failing, not understanding something, and upsetting people, in no particular order. You have a fierce fondness for fairness, rules and order. You have a lot of gates and you are extremely conscious, and self-conscious, of them all, and those of others. You're not a big fan of confrontation, so you invented passive-aggressive. You found your niche quickly – that is, being quite good – and you applied yourself to all subjects, regardless of being the worst artist in the universe. You had preselected your path of most likely success from the table before you, and you ran with it. The world was yours for the exploration, and your career path was broad. Yet it was never really about the path you chose, but how you navigate your way along it. Success does not mean power, prestige or wads of cash. You are always more concerned about parameters than pastimes or positions. You see the world in a big way, especially the older you get. And you change jobs a fair amount, often in the same fields – civil service, public service, social service, teaching, nursing, research, policy and planning – as you have an innate desire to see those parameters in action in different contexts, and do your part for the larger purpose of humanity. And your spelling and grammar is good, often stunning. You feel sorry for Matt, but can see the causes and could explain the complications without swearing as much as the Blues. You were born straight into the mainstream whether you realised it or not.

You are Red. You are brilliant in some ways. Your maths and science skills are off the charts and you can write very neatly, technically and coherently, and you enjoy reading. You are easily annoyed by others, yet focused. Weakness of character exasperates you. Poor choices agitate you. Money matters, but it hasn't consumed your life. You are comfortable, not filthy rich.

You wear decent clothes. Appearance matters more than most. You are a high-flyer and you don't mind being surrounded by others of the same ilk – this is your thrill. The ladder can never be high enough. You have plenty of stuff, but occasionally want more. You can afford it. You are an expert in a particular field and your views are respected, if not revered. Your team works hard because you work hard. You are in charge because you always wanted to be. You are the executive director, the surgeon, the head of the company, the top of the class, the top brass. You have been head-hunted for different roles. You are known; you want to be known. You have singular objectives and you have hired and fired people. You have a number of gates, but you can move through them at your convenience and expedience – they are yours to open at will. You heard about Matt on the news, but you have never done his kind of work and cannot readily relate. It doesn't affect you and you don't give it all a second thought. You were born into a fast-flowing mainstream, sink or swim, and you swam hard. Now the purpose of that water is to take you where you want to go – it's a destination, not a journey. You are the focus. Your path is clear. You're on your way.

Whether or not you see yourself (or your career) in any of these descriptions doesn't matter – it's not a test. We sometimes sit at all of those tables, but we do gravitate towards one more than the others. It's not about being right, which after all is being observational and opinionated. And we cannot observe more than what we can see around us, with our opinions often being little more than stating the obvious.

So if you want to be a turquoise unicorn, no one can stop you. Yet if you don't mind defining yourself broadly within the mainstream, and recognise your trends and tendencies to maintaining its existence, or not, you have a frame of reference at the very least. If you can't see the frame, you're not in the mainstream. If you can see the frame but want to destroy it, you are dangerous. For minority opinion exists within every group, and every group has contributed, and will contribute, to the state of our societies, at every level of the concrete and the conscious. So are you here to protect or pollute the mainstream? In light of all that has come before you, and all that lies ahead of you, what on earth are you thinking? What on earth are you doing? Who are you, really?

No arrow flies in a perfectly straight line. There is an arc in the archer's bow, as well as an arch. We are all subject to forces before us, behind us, above us and below us. We are all supports and all need supports. The more we stray from the mainstream, from the middle, the less support we provide and the more support we demand. It is only when we are shoulder to shoulder that our arches stay true to their function and work for the good of us all. We are only truly united by what makes us the same. Diversity provides colour, never clarity.

Our first frame of reference has always been each other. It starts with kin and expands outwards, but always comes back to kin. When we are forced to stand in places unfamiliar, and with people who are not kin; when that process is not natural nor organic, we are uncomfortable, twitchy, faking it. Our shoulders constantly rub, but never lock in. Our decision-making suffers; our societies lose their direction. They lose their edges and their edge. They can no longer define who they are. They stand upon shifting sands.

It takes very little in the way of effort to destroy a framework compared to the tremendous endeavour needed in keeping it intact. Yet it requires more force to get something moving than it does to keep it moving. If all we are doing is continually starting again, without reason or rationale, all we're doing is wasting time and energy. We don't need to destroy everything as there's nothing new under the sun. Our frameworks are there to be evaluated, further engineered and made better, not shattered into dust. We can work with the forces at play if we put our minds to it. Things can be mended on the fly, patched together; holes can be plugged, gaps filled in. Once that boat sets sail and you can't anchor or find safe harbour, you keep going. And when your course is altered by a storm, you find direction again using tried and tested methods based on ancient understanding. When your GPS is out of range, the stars can align you. The light is ever there to guide your way, day or night. We are all at sea.

If you find yourself screaming at the world you don't have a plan. There are no plans on the fringes of thought, just chaos incarnate. If you crossed a line, can you come back? If you can't see the fence, your only frame of reference is the echo of your own voice in the darkness, and the cries of others mixing with your own. You aren't really a group, but you can move together, and swell like the tide, but you are just a bunch of people shrieking together, whatever you call yourselves or however you mobilise. A movement is not kin. A mob is not kin. It's not a plan that works, regardless of how much good you think you are doing by the damage you are doing. You don't even see it as damage. You're not being good.

And if you want to be that turquoise unicorn, you're still a unicorn, in a room full of unicorns. You can splinter your identity further and demand new titles and new concessions, but even you can't keep up with that. You'll find yourself further and further away from the reasons why you wanted to be a turquoise unicorn in the first place – to be accepted, loved, liked for who you are. But you loathe who you are more than you think and in doing so find yourself loathed, even when you're not. You were accepted by the majority. They liked the quirkiness of you and most had adapted to the changes, often opening their most stiffened of gates to let the process move along. But you didn't give them the time and tried to smash their gates before they got there, in order for it all to work immediately for you; and while they forgave you for this, you never forgave yourself, but blamed them all for your guilt and shame anyway. That was the only plan you had, if you ever thought you had one. You didn't.

And what of risk? Did you choose to eliminate it for others without asking them how they felt about their own choices? You curtailed their harm, even before they had a chance to try their hand, and they never learned the hard way. You chose not to frustrate their minds. But all learning is hard, or it isn't learning. And in the end you only caused the frustration to manifest itself all at once, piled up in a great heap, and it swept upon them and swept them away. They lost sight of where they were and now they cannot easily find their way back, as there are no markers, no fixed points of progress, no process, no problem-solving, no gates. You flung them into chaos because you thought you were doing good, and now they are drowning in the shallow end, even though you made the deep end off limits. Yet you still updated your vitae with the wonderful progress you had made.

In whatever role you find yourself – priest, principal, prophet, poet, politician, pundit, peasant farmer – you have sat at a table, and you still sit at a table. Beside you and around you are your new kin. In forgotten days and distant times where all work and play was with kin, we are now thrust together in the melting pot, the mosaic, the muddled tapestry of all our national and global aspirations, blended as if as one beneath ever-gathering clouds. Our voices mix and mingle: shrill and soft, coarse and calm, fervent and furtive; our ideas intertwine and overlap, spilling out and spilling over. The boundaries that once we knew, deeply, intrinsically, are lost to the growing tides of change and decay, but we feel them and we miss them, and we can never get them back.

We mourn for what we've lost and pretend to care for what we've gained, because we're told to, because we're taught to, because we're trained to. We test ourselves on our new knowledge and measure ourselves by our new righteousness; arguing, quarrelling, quibbling, squabbling over trivia, over things we just made up, over frameworks we bent, twisted and burned to the ground, over lies, truths, facts, fiction. We flitted and flirted with chaos because we hated who we were and what we had; we never really settled, even the settlers. We conquered ourselves. We lost our kin.

We cannot do good; we can only look back and pick through the rubble, hoping that something or someone survived; and we display these stories to the world, these snippets, trinkets, tiny testaments of hope, as proofs of our righteous purpose and onward, progressive momentum. Yet we make our beds in the darkness and slumber in the day, stricken by our false positives, stunned by our achievements. We see advancement, improvement, shine – hand in hand with retreat, decline and corrosion. We are ever at a crossroads, uncertain which path to take and which path got us there in the first place.

We are terrified of nothing, doing nothing, silence. We fill our days with noise, fuss, fanfare and fun – our diversity keeps us occupied, but rarely satisfied. We jostle and jiggle for position, for definition, for a new place on the board. We drown our sorrows by drowning ourselves, and our sorrows remained where they always were, only now transferred to our kin, and translated into new forms of heartache and melancholy, agony and anguish, passed down from generation to generation, handed out on a platter full of decaying food. We soiled our own linens and desecrated our own tables, gorging ourselves on the bounties of the world and vomiting at the excess. We ridiculed and ravaged the ancient grounds, urging ourselves onward to gain even more, ripping the heart out of nature's benevolence and defiling the purest of spaces with greed and gluttony. We sacrificed it all to gain the end of the rainbow. We gave ourselves no chance. What chance did we give others?

We stand on the edge of night, bested by the worst of us, beaten by the best of us; hoping, calling, crying, falling, falling, falling.

We are all slain.

# Epilogue

There is a fundamental difference between being good and doing good. Being good is a state of mind, body and spirit; doing good is an undertaking of the conscious self. To *be* good, you abstain and avoid. To *do* good, you apply yourself and act.

If we ask ourselves if we are being good, what do we mean by the question? How does being good produce good results if it's only a state of mind, body and spirit? It flies in the face of conventional wisdom, surely? There was never any such wisdom.

Being good is not asceticism. It is not isolation, nor hibernation. Hermits aren't being good simply because they hide themselves away from the world. You could be the most nefarious human in existence and still become a hermit, albeit we would all appreciate that choice. We'd rather the really bad people take themselves off quietly into a lonely corner and not show themselves ever again. It's why we invented jails, because such people don't tend to self-isolate very well.

Instead, in our fractured world, we try to be good in different ways, and share those ways with others. We like to make it obvious and apparent. If folding pillowcases like a guru is being good, it becomes a mini-series. If poking little needles behind our ears and into other painful crevices is an ancient goodness for body and soul, we do it. We are always seeking ways to be good, particularly for ourselves, and that is what it is supposed to be. You can't "be" good for someone else, at least not directly. The only time where that is important is for our children – they need to be good, and learn to be good, so that when they are older the sum total of their behaviour leans towards the righteous. They'll still do stupid things, as we all do, but more good will come from what they do rather than bad. The balance of the eternal scales always tips in favour of the good if we are being that way to begin with. The words "being" and "begin" contain the same letters, after all, which is a rather appropriate coincidence.

And that is, and always has been, the crux of it all. The fabric of our existence comes down to simple acts of being, and there is no one-size-fits-all handbook. Every culture has its own means and methods to be good, some more bizarre and arcane than others, but we can all become aware of them if we ask, and if we entertain the reasons and the notions for why those things are done, and have been done for aeons. We already try some of these things out, but need to expand our horizons and have more conversations and consults with each other – kin to kin, clan to clan, culture to culture. We can't be forced to like everything that the other does, but we can find that common ground, that unity in our innate sameness. And for the love of God can we please stop bleating on about getting along just because we are different and celebrating those unique things for the sake of it. I am quite sure the majority have had enough of that nonsense. We've been hammering those large, square pegs into little round holes for long enough. All it does is tear the fabric of who we are. Matt is fully on board with this plan, bless him. (He got a new job by the way, did I mention that?)

There can be no greater purpose for anyone than serving a purpose greater than themselves. Love itself would agree with this. Bound to our essence, aside from all the fakery, forgery and failure of our nature, lies an elemental desire to help, to cure, to save, to soothe, to heal. We're not completely awful, but we can be. The choice was ever up to us. It's not about being all we can be, or being who we are, whatever those ghastly catchphrases are even supposed to mean, but being without sin. Yes, the preaching is in full flow here and you may be glad this is the Epilogue. I wouldn't blame you, which is what we do well, even me. What "sin" is for you is your own determination – we can all point it out in others – but there is significant evidence to suggest than an absence of it in your life, my life, our lives, will be very good for us indeed. That really and truly is being good.

We are all still slain, but light is an everlasting thing.

# Postscript

od doesn't create chaos: he inherits it, and so do we. The moment our squirmy, slimy little bodies are delivered from the womb, we are born into a world of it. And over the course of our days we strive for order, routine, schedule, familiarity, happiness and rest. We yearn for better relationships with each other and the world we inhabit, constantly seeking to establish clear direction in the midst of the madness.

Yet our history is not the fable of perfection gone wrong that requires us putting right. It is not a tale of an Eden to be reimagined by mortal minds. It is not a paradise waiting to be recreated, by our hands or otherwise. The apple has been eaten. The bell has sounded. The song has been sung. What happened cannot be untasted, unheard or unserenaded. We stand as if on the brink of a void, into which every hope, dream, plan and promise evaporates and endlessly swirls in the nebulous fogs of doubt and despair.

But Light screams through the maelstrom. It carves an in-eradicable path between and beyond the turmoil of darkness; scorching, blistering, burning away the hidden foulness of endless night. It needs no keys, it is the Key, and it shatters every ancient chain, every filth-encrusted shackle, and breaks apart forever every rusted, heartless bar of iron. It penetrates every depth, every chasm, every putrid cell, and releases, reveals; relentless in its course.  It cannot be stopped, it cannot be shielded, it cannot be unmade. And it makes all, unmakes all that has been made, and brings anew the source of all life, in all ways, and for all eternity.

We were slain, once.

And then, reborn.

*The End*

# Dedication (Part II)

I didn't have any choice.

*~ for my Mum and Dad ~*

May God bless you both now, and forever, unto the heights of heaven.

www.ingramcontent.com/pod-product-compliance
Lightning Source LLC
Chambersburg PA
CBHW051452250726
48655CB00001B/376